Landscapes of
LANZAROTE
a countryside guide

Noel Rochford

SUNFLOWER
BOOKS

Dedicated to Augustín Pallarés Padilla

Revised printing 1994.
First published 1989 by
Sunflower Books
12 Kendrick Mews
London SW7 3HG, UK

Verode

ISBN 1-85691-037-7

Important note to the reader

I have tried to ensure that the descriptions and maps in this book are error-free at press date. The book will be updated, where necessary, whenever future printings permit. It will be very helpful for me to receive your comments (sent in care of the publishers, please) for the updating of future printings. I also rely on those who use this book — especially walkers — to take along a good supply of common sense when they explore. Conditions change fairly rapidly on Lanzarote, and *storm damage or bulldozing may make a route unsafe at any time.* If the route is not as I outline it here, and your way ahead is not secure, return to the point of departure. ***Never attempt to complete a tour or walk under hazardous conditions!*** Please read carefully the notes on pages 7 to 13, as well as the introductory comments at the beginning of each tour and walk (regarding road conditions, equipment, grade, distances and time, etc). Explore *safely*, while at the same time respecting the beauty of the countryside.

Photographs by the author
Maps by John Theasby and Pat Underwood
Drawings by Sharon Rochford
Printed and bound in the UK by KPC Group, Ashford, Kent
6 5 4 3 2 1

❀ Contents

Teguise

 Preface

Within just a few years, Lanzarote has grown from a quiet, relatively unknown tourist resort to an island buzzing with some 600,000 tourists annually. Fortunately, these visitors are confined to three fairly small areas, and the rest of the island remains blissfully rural and unspoilt.

Few holidaymakers realise that Lanzarote has more to offer than just beaches and sunshine. I was sceptical. When my publisher suggested Lanzarote for my next book, I felt sure that I was doing penance for past manuscripts. But a pleasant surprise awaited me.

This fascinating 797-square-kilometre island is truly extraordinary. Its fate was decided some two and one-half centuries ago, when the largest volcanic eruption in recorded history took place, leaving a strange and alluring countryside in its wake — a landscape littered with volcanoes and dark streams of jagged lava. This is the backdrop to nearly every scene on the island, and intriguing sights abound, as you can see from the photographs in this book.

If you were to suggest walking on Lanzarote to most visitors, they would think you mad. "Where is there to walk?" But I can think of no better place in the Canary Islands for just strolling. No doubt 'serious' walkers will find Tenerife and Gran Canaria, for example, more challenging, but ramblers will be in their element on Lanzarote. Each of the walks in this book takes you to a different corner of the island and shows you a scenically-different outlook. But if walking is not your favourite pastime, then *do* rent a vehicle of sorts and explore on wheels. Use the book to reach places off the beaten track and see another face of Lanzarote.

At present all eyes are on this island. Will it indeed set an example in preservation, or will it follow in the footsteps of Tenerife and Gran Canaria, falling prey to the concrete of greedy developers? Fortunately, Lanzarote has one advantage over the other islands. It is the home of the well-known artist-designer — and, more importantly, conservationist — César Manrique. Together with his supporters, he is working to preserve the island's environmental heritage.

I hope this new addition to the *Landscapes* Series convinces you that there is much more to Lanzarote than beaches and sunshine.

Acknowledgements

My thanks to the following people, who helped me with the preparation of the material on Lanzarote:

Señor Francisco Ortega, Director, Patronato Insular de Turismo de Lanzarote;

Servicio Geográfico del Ejercito, Madrid, for permission to adapt their maps;

Señores Carlos Gutierrez Gutierrez and Norberto Palomino Gallego, for additional military maps;

ICONA;

Jackie, for her errands.

Very special thanks to Augustín Pallarés Padilla for invaluable suggestions and for hours spent answering my questions; and to my sister Sharon, for her splendid drawings.

Finally, thanks to my family, friends, and publishers, who always support my work and travels.

Useful books

Bramwell, D and Bramwell, Z *Wild Flowers of the Canary Islands.* Stanley Thornes Ltd.

Bramwell, D and Bramwell, Z *Historia Natural de las Islas Canarias.* Editorial Rueda.

Vicente Araña and Juán Carracedo, *Los volcanes de las Islas Canarias, II: Lanzarote y Fuerteventura* (with English text). Editorial Rueda.

Prickly pear

❀ Introduction

Getting about on the island

The best way to get around Lanzarote is by **hired car.** This can be very economical, especially when you hire a car for a few days or a week. **Taxis** are only economical if shared, and all fares should be ascertained in advance. *Note: Never* leave anything of value in your car. Lock your personal belongings in the boot, or carry them with you. Thefts from cars are not uncommon. Always try to park where there are other cars and people are about.

Coach tours are easy to arrange and get you to all the tourist points of interest, but never off the beaten track. The **local bus service** is very limited outside Puerto del Carmen and Costa de Teguise; it serves the school children and villagers. Most of the walks in this book can be reached by local bus, however — with departures from Arrecife. **Bus timetables** are shown on the touring map. *Don't* rely solely on these, however. As soon as you arrive on the island, update these timetables by getting 'first-hand' information from the *bus station* (it's best *not* to rely on tourist office handouts). See town plans (with the touring map) for bus stops and stations in both Arrecife and Puerto del Carmen. The buses may run late, but you should *always arrive about fifteen minutes early.* In the Arrecife bus station it will take you that long to find out *which one* is your bus!

Picnicking

Picnicking isn't one of Lanzarote's strong points. Shade is the biggest problem — there are not many trees on the island! Nor are there any 'organised' picnic sites, as there are on other Canary Islands. If you have just one day for picnicking, don't miss Picnic 2 (Risco de Famara). I think this is one of the loveliest and most memorable places to enjoy a picnic in the entire archipelago.

On pages 14 and 15 you will find my suggestions for eight lovely picnic spots, together with all the information you need to reach them. *Note that picnic numbers correspond to walk numbers*; thus you can quickly find the general location on the island by referring to the pull-out touring map (where the walk locations are shown in white). Most of the spots I've chosen are very easy to reach, and I outline transport details (🚐 = bus information; 🚗 = car or taxi parking), walking times, and views or setting. Beside the picnic title, you'll also find a map reference: the exact location of the picnic spot is shown on this large-scale *walking* map by the symbol *P*. Some of the picnic areas are also illustrated; if so, the photograph reference follows the map reference.

Please glance over the comments before you start off on your picnic: if some walking is involved, remember to wear sensible shoes and to **take a sunhat** (☼ = picnic in full sun). It's a good idea to take along a plastic groundsheet as well, in case the ground is damp.

If you are travelling to your picnic by bus, be sure to verify departure times in advance. Although there are timetables in this book, they *do* change from time to time, without prior warning. **If you are travelling to your picnic by car**, be extra vigilant off the main roads.

All picnickers should read the country code on page 13 and go quietly in the countryside. *Buen provecho!*

Touring

Hiring a vehicle is such good value on Lanzarote that it would be a pity not to take advantage of it. Do shop around first, however, while at the same time bearing in mind that cheapest is not always best! Always check your vehicle in advance and point out any existing dents, scratches, etc. Ask for all the conditions and insurance cover in writing, in English. Check to make sure you have a sound spare tyre and all the necessary tools. Be sure to get the office *and the after-hours* telephone numbers of the hire firm and carry them with you. If you're not 100% happy about the car, don't take it. Finally, make a note of exactly what you're signing for, if you pay by credit card

You *can* tour Lanzarote in just one day without missing any of the main sights (indicated with a ★ in the touring notes and on the touring map) ... as long as you make a *very* early start.

The touring notes are brief: they contain little history or information readily available in tourist office leaflets (which you can obtain free of charge). The main tourist centres and towns are not described either, for the same reason. Instead, I concentrate on the 'logistics' of touring: times and distances, road conditions, and seeing places many tourists miss. Most of all I emphasise possibilities for walking and picnicking. While some of the references to picnics off the beaten track (indicated by the symbol **P** in the touring notes) may not be suitable during a long car tour, you may see a landscape that you would like to explore at leisure another day, when you've more time to stretch your legs.

The large fold-out touring map is designed to be held out opposite the touring notes and contains all the information you will need outside the towns. The tours have been written up starting from Puerto del Carmen, but you can join them from other points quite easily. **Town plans** with exits for motorists are on the touring map. Remember to allow plenty of time for **visits**, and to take along **warm clothing** as well as some food and drink, in case you are delayed. The **distances** quoted in the notes are *cumulative* from the departure point. A **key to symbols** used in the touring notes on pages 16 to 30 is on the touring map.

All motorists should read the country code on page 13 and go quietly in the countryside. *Buen viaje!*

Walking

While Lanzarote may not be the destination you might choose, were you planning a walking holiday, you will be as surprised as I was to find what this island has to offer walkers and nature lovers.

The walks in this book cover a good cross-section of the island. Do them all, and you will *almost* know Lanzarote inside-out. *Almost* — because, in a very commendable attempt to preserve the beauty of the island, the government will not permit you to explore the Timanfaya National Park on your own; you'll have to join the coach-trippers.

There are walks in this book for everyone. To choose a walk that appeals to you, you might begin by looking at the touring map inside the back cover. Here you can see at a glance the overall terrain, the roads, and the location of the walks. Flipping through the book, you will see that there is at least one photograph for every walk. Having selected one or two potential excursions from the map and the photographs, turn to the relevant walk. At the top of the page you will find planning information: distance/time, grade, equipment, and how to get there. If the grade and equipment specifications are beyond your scope, don't despair! *There's almost always a short or alternative version of a walk,* and in most cases these are far less demanding. *If you want a really easy walk, you need look no further than the picnic suggestions on pages 14 and 15.* For the hardy among you, look no further than Walk 2; this will get you huffing and puffing!

When you are on your walk, you will find that the text begins with an introduction to the landscape and then turns to a detailed description of the route. The **large-scale maps** (generally 1:40,000 or 1:50,000) have been annotated to show key landmarks. Times are given for reaching certain points in the walk. **Note: I am a very fit, very fast walker!** So if you are a beginner, or if you prefer a more leisurely pace, a walk may **take you more than twice as long!** The most imporant factor is *consistency* of times, and I suggest that you compare your pace with mine on one or two short walks, before you set off on a long hike. Don't forget to take bus connections into account!

Note that roads and tracks on the walking **maps** correspond to those on the touring map. The **main walk route** is shown by a solid green line, alternative routes by a dashed green line. A **scale** of miles/kilometres is on each map. Below is a key to the symbols used:

☎	best views	*P*	picnic spot (see page 7)
⚲/✛	church, chapel/shrine	⚡	danger; danger of vertigo!
◀●	spring, tank, etc	⇔	car parking
◻◻◻	habitations	■	building in the text
⚡	pylon, wires	▬	walls (usually stone)

Dogs and other nuisances

Dogs are a nuisance, that's for sure! They can recognise a softie a mile off, and they would follow me to the end of the walk. No amount of threatening or abuse deterred them. That's the only 'nuisance' on Lanzarote.

Weather

With an average annual temperature of 21°C and less than 140mm (5½ inches) of rain per year, Lanzarote has about 125 days of sunshine. You can't go wrong on a winter holiday here. You may strike a few bad days, but the only place where the weather could ruin your day would be in the north, where low cloud might prevent you from appreciating those superb seascapes. It would be very rare for rain to disrupt an entire day on the island. Rain usually lasts for only an hour or two, and then the sun shines again. Fortunately for walkers, there are some cool and cloudy days — these are not as uncommon as the tourist brochures would lead you to believe. The winter months (November to March) are best for walking, but even then the days can be hot.

A few facts and figures: Temperatures average between 14-21°C in winter and 18-28°C in summer, with humidity reaching between 60-70%. Good news for windsurfers: Lanzarote is a relatively windy island, with the *alisio* (trade winds) blowing for much of the year, and the mean average water temperature is 20°C.

In spring and summer there are occasional days when a warm wind blows from Africa, bringing with it fine particles of dust. It's not very pleasant, as the temperatures can be quite high, but it only lasts a few days.

Where to stay

Most of you will be staying in one of three places: Puerto del Carmen (the tourist capital), Costa de Teguise (smaller and classier), or Playa Blanca (still in its infancy). Any of these bases is fine, provided that you have a hired vehicle. However, if walking is more important to you than is the beach, and you are not planning to hire a car, it would be best to base yourself in Arrecife, from where you can easily get to all the walks by local bus. Puerto del Carmen *does* have a regular bus connection with Arrecife, but bear in mind that the service returning *from* Puerto del Carmen to Arrecife is not always strictly to the timetable. Costa de Teguise has a limited service connecting with Arrecife, and the service from Playa Blanca to the capital is only once a day each way.

All three tourist centres are within reach of at least three walks in the book, and you will find that by sharing a taxi one way and taking a local bus for the other part of the route (since you can usually get a bus at least one way), the cost for getting to and returning from walks is not high.

What to take

If you're already on Lanzarote when you find this book, and you don't have any special equipment such as walking boots or a rucksack, you can still do some of the walks — or buy yourself some equipment in one of the sports shops. Don't attempt the more difficult walks without the proper gear. For each walk in the book, the *minimum* equipment is listed.

Please bear in mind that I've not done *every* walk in this book under *all* weather conditions. Use your good judgement to modify my equipment list according to the season! You may find the following checklist useful:

walking boots (which *must* be broken-in and comfortable)	up-to-date transport timetables
waterproof rain gear (outside summer months)	lightweight water containers
	extra pair of socks
long-sleeved shirt (sun protection)	long trousers, tight at the ankles
bandages and band-aids	protective sun cream
plastic plates, cups, etc	knives and openers
anorak (zip opening)	2 lightweight cardigans
spare bootlaces	plastic groundsheet
sunhat	whistle
insect repellant	compass
small rucksack	torch

Spanish for walkers and motorists

In the tourist centres you hardly need know any Spanish. But out in the countryside, a few words of the language will be helpful, especially if you lose your way.

Here's an — almost — foolproof way to communicate in Spanish. First, memorise the few short key questions and their possible answers, given below. Then, when you have your 'mini-speech' memorised, always ask the many questions you can concoct from it **in such a way that you get a "sí" (yes) or "no" answer.** *Never* ask an open-ended question such as "Where is the main road?". Instead, ask the question and then *suggest the most likely answer yourself.* For instance: "Good day, sir. Please — where is the path to Máguez? *Is it straight ahead?*" Now, unless you get a "sí" response, try: "*Is it to the left?*" If you go through the list of answers to your own question, you will eventually get a "sí" response, and this is more reassuring than relying solely on sign language.

Following are the most likely situations in which you may have to practice your Spanish. The dots (...) show where you will fill in the name of your destination. Ask a local person — perhaps someone at your hotel — to help you with place name pronunciation.

Asking the way
Key questions

English	Spanish	Pronunciation
Good day,	Buenos días,	**Boo**-eh-nohs **dee**-ahs,
sir (madam, miss).	señor (señora, señorita).	sen-**yor** (sen-**yor**-ah, sen-yor-**ee**-tah).
Please —	Por favor —	**Poor** fah-**vor** —
where is	dónde está	**dohn**-day es-**tah**
the road to ...?	la carretera a ...?	lah cah-reh-**teh**-rah ah ...?
the footpath to...?	la senda de ...?	lah **sen**-dah day ...?
the way to ...?	el camino a ...?	el cah-**mee**-noh ah ...?
the bus stop?	la parada?	lah pah-**rah**-dah?
Many thanks.	Muchas gracias.	**Moo**-chas **gra**-thee-ahs.

Possible answers

English	Spanish	Pronunciation
here?	aquí?	ah-**kee**?
there?	allá?	ayl-**yah**?
straight ahead?	todo recto?	**toh**-doh **rayk**-toh?
behind?	detrás?	day-**tras**?
right?	a la derecha?	ah lah day-**ray**-chah?
left?	a la izquierda?	ah lah eeth-kee-**er**-dah?
above?	arriba?	ah-**ree**-bah?
below?	abajo?	ah-**bah**-hoh?

Asking a taxidriver to take you somewhere and return for you, or asking a taxi driver to meet you at a certain place and time

English	Spanish	Pronunciation
Please —	Por favor —	**Poor** fah-**vor** —
take us to ...	llévanos a ...	**l-yay**-vah-nohs ah...
and return	y venga buscarnos	ee **vain**-gah boos-**kar**-nohs
at (place) at (time).	a ... a ... .*	ah (place) ah (time).*

*Just point out the time on your watch.

A country code for walkers and motorists

- **Do not light fires.**
- **Do not frighten animals.** The goats and sheep you may encounter on your walks are not tame.
- **Walk quietly** through all hamlets and villages.
- **Leave all gates just as you find them.** Although you may not see any animals, the gates *do* have a purpose — generally to keep goats or sheep in (or out of) an area.
- **Protect all wild and cultivated plants.** Don't try to pick wild flowers or uproot saplings. Obviously fruit and other crops are someone's private property and should not be touched. *Never walk over cultivated land.*
- **Take all your litter away with you.**
- **Walkers — *Do not take risks!*** This is the most important point of all. Do not attempt walks beyond your capacity, and do not wander off the paths described here if there is any sign of mist or if it is late in the day. **Do not walk alone**, and *always* tell a responsible person *exactly* where you are going and what time you plan to return. Remember, if you become lost or injure yourself, it may be a long time before you are found. On any but a very short walk close to villages, be sure to take a compass, whistle, torch, extra water and warm clothing — as well as some high-energy food, like chocolate. Read and re-read the important note on page 2, as well as the guidelines on grade and equipment for each walk you plan to do!

Vinagrera

Picnic suggestions

1 LA GRACIOSA (map page 33)

by 🚤: 20-25min on foot. Ferry from Orzola to La Graciosa.
Off the ferry, skirt the waterfront to your left and continue around in front of and through the houses on the shore. Beyond the houses come to a superb beach and shortly after, a tidal lagoon. It's a fantastic spot, from where you look across to the impressive Risco de Famara (see Picnic 2). ✪

2 RISCO DE FAMARA (map page 40, photographs pages 17 and 37)

by 🚗 *only:* 5-10min on foot. Park by the side of the road, 1.5km southwest of the Mirador del Río: Descending off the plateau, you come into cultivated fields. You'll see two derelict stone buildings set just below the side of the road. A dyke (a natural wall of rock) cuts across to the right directly behind them and, immediately beyond it, a track forks off right into the fields (alongside the dyke). Turn off onto the track and follow it to the end — or, if the track is too rough, park alongside the buildings.
Sit on the ledge of the cliff, below the track, and overlook the Mirador del Río vista — now you'll have the view all to yourself. No other picnic site on the island matches this one. Cliffs provide the only shade. ✪

3 MAGUEZ (map page 40, photograph page 22)

by 🚌: 30-35min on foot. Bus to Máguez.
by 🚗 : 20-25min on foot. On entering Máguez *from the north*, you en-counter a fork in the road: bear left and, a few hundred metres/yards along, see a track bearing off to the left. Park on the side of the road here, without obstructing traffic.

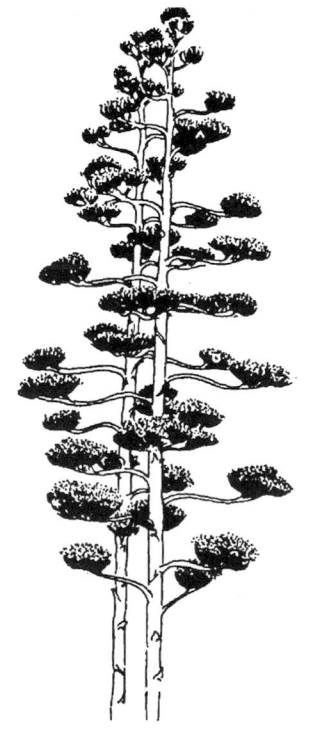

Set off along the farm track, following the notes at the bottom of page 39 up to where the text reads 'just over 20min from Máguez ... we cross an intersection'. Here you can picnic on the grassy hillock above. There is a lovely view over the cultivated slopes down to the east coast, and Montaña Corona stands just behind you. ✪

4 PICO DE LAS NIEVES (map page 44)

by 🚗 *only:* 0-5min on foot. Park by the chapel at Pico de las Nieves, off the GC700.
Picnic anywhere on the top of the crest. The views across the centre of the Lanzarote and out to its neighbouring islands are mag-nificent. ✪

American aloe

6 MONTAÑA GUARDILAMA (map page 53, photographs pages 51, 53, 54)

Lavandula pinnata

by 🚌: 35-40min on foot. Bus to Uga.

by 🚗: 5-15min on foot. Turn off the Uga—Teguise road some 600m/yds past the junction north of Uga, onto the first track forking off east. Park off the side of the road at the entrance to the track; don't block the track. If you travel by jeep, you can drive up to the pass (this would take 40 minutes on foot).

Use the notes on pages 50- 52 to reach the pass, or go as far as you wish up the track. You have a superb view over the dark Geria Valley — quite a sight when the vines are coming into leaf. ☻

7 ATALAYA DE FEMÉS (map page 56, photograph page 57)

by 🚗 *only:* 30-40min on foot. Park in Femés.
Use the map for Walk 7, page 56. Follow the dirt track that leaves from behind the church and climbs the Atalaya de Femés. Picnic off the track above the first crater (from where your views will be limited), or carry on to the summit another 15 minutes further up. From there you will have an excellent view of the volcanoes of Timanfaya and the south of the island — as well as the northern part of Fuerteventura. Note that this is a strenuous climb, and it can be very windy and cool! ☻

8 JANUBIO (map page 60, photographs pages 59, 60)

by 🚌: 40-45min on foot. Bus to La Hoya.
by 🚗: 5-10min on foot. Turn off the Playa Blanca road onto the track signposted 'Playa', some 800m/yds beyond the junction for El Golfo. If approaching from Puerto del Carmen, this is the *second* track off right. Park above the beach.
Either picnic on this black sand beach or follow the walk notes on page 59 to head along the coastline to the left. There you'll find a choice spot amidst the rock fringing the shore. The beautiful rock pools lie between 40-50 minutes along. ☻

9 PLAYA DE PAPAGAYO (map pages 62-63, photograph page 64)

by 🚗 *only:* 0-5min on foot. Follow the gravel road east out of Playa Blanca (there are no signposts, and sections of road are under construction). Playa de Papagayo lies at the end of the main gravel road, 6km out (ignore the numerous branch-offs). Park around the hamlet above the beach.
Expect company here: Playa de Papagayo is mentioned in all the guides. There are good spots in the cove or on the rocky promontory to the right of the beach. Punta del Papagayo, less than 10 minutes beyond the hamlet, is always quiet. This point is usually windy. Playa de Puerto Muelas and the other beaches lining the coast also make splendid picnic spots. ☻

☻ Reminder: Little or **no** shade!

1 THE SIGHTS OF THE NORTH

Puerto del Carmen • Tahiche • Arrieta • Jameos del Agua • Cueva de los Verdes • Orzola • Mirador del Río • Haría • Teguise • La Caleta • Mozaga • Puerto del Carmen

140km/87mi; about 3h30min driving; Exit A from Puerto del Carmen

On route: ***P*** (see pages 14-15) 2, 3, 4; Walks 2, 3, 4

Roads are generally good, but often narrow. The road from Cueva de los Verdes to the GC710 (3km) is exceedingly narrow. Some motorists may find the roads around the Mirador del Río unnerving — especially near the Famara cliffs: there is at present no roadside railing. Cloud and mist are not infrequent in the northern hills, and visibility can be reduced to almost zero! Look out for livestock on the roads and for pedestrians in the villages. A slow speed is recommended for these roads. Note: There is only one petrol station between Arrieta and Mozaga — some 90km. Note also that some petrol stations are closed on Sundays and holidays. Arrecife is not included in this tour because it is well served by public transport and may be visited another day.

Important: *Although driving time is only three and one-half hours, allow an entire day for this tour if you want to visit all the tourist attractions.*

Opening hours:
Jameos del Agua: 11.00-19.30 daily
Cueva de los Verdes: 11.00-18.00 daily
Museo Sacro de Haría: 11.00-13.00 daily
Mirador del Río (bar): 11.00-19.00 daily
Castillo de Santa Bárbara: 10.00-18.00 daily
Palacio de Spínola: 10.00-13.00 and 16.00-18.00 daily

O utside of the Timanfaya National Park, the northern part of Lanzarote is the most scenically interesting. As you follow this tour, winding your way around and over the northern massif, you'll encounter the extraordinarily beautiful colours, shapes and textures that create the landscape canvas of Lanzarote. You'll need lots of film for your camera! Cueva de los Verdes — a vast volcanic tube measuring one kilometre in length, may be the most intriguing cave you've ever seen. You'll also learn who César Manrique is and what he means to the island — or, rather, what his native land means to him.

We leave Puerto del Carmen by heading north on the Avenida de las Playas (Exit A). On joining the main south road (GC720) bear right and, 4km along — just beyond a petrol station — turn off onto the circular road that skirts Arrecife. Next we turn off onto the GC700 and head for Tahiche/Teguise. Now the tour really begins.

At **Tahiche** (20km ✹) we take the GC710 for Orzola, passing through an open flat countryside pierced by prominent isolated hills. Approaching the Moorish-flavoured village of **Guatiza** (▲▲ 29km) we come into cultivated fields and gardens squared off by stone walls. The village itself is swallowed up amidst fields of prickly pear. Leaving the village, pass the cactus garden (**Jardín de Cactus★**; still under construction at press date) on your right. A well-preserved windmill stands above it. Soon the entire plain is taken over by prickly pear. Farmed pricky pear is an unusual sight — normally we see it growing wild. The cochineal insect is bred on these

The fabulous setting of the Mirador del Río (Tour 1). The cliff is the famous Risco de Famara — see Walk 2.

plants: the female lives off the juice of the cactus leaf, and after three months is harvested and dried in the sun. Today cochineal is used as colouring in lipsticks, toothpastes, and some drinks — Campari, for instance. The dye was once important in the carpet industry and, during the last century, was a major money-earner for Lanzarote.

Off the sea-plain you look up into ridges that trail off the northern hills. **Mala** (32km ✖; starting point for Walk 4), another spacious farming village, follows. The 'Lanzarote colours' can be seen in the white façades and green doorways and window shutters of the houses. Passing **Arrieta** (37km ▢✖▲), a small seaside village built along the rocky shore, head straight through the junction. Then bear right immediately for Jameos del Agua and Cueva de los Verdes. A few minutes before you reach the turn-off to Jameos del Agua, you pass **Punta Mujeres** (38km ✖), a tight cluster of dwellings with more than its fair share of restaurants. Some 4km from Arrieta we branch off for **Jameos del Agua★** (42km ✖), one of the island's most-frequented tourist attractions. This enchanting cave is the result of two opposing forces — man and nature. A splendid compromise has been reached: the eruption of Montaña Corona is responsible for the natural element;

In Timanfaya National Park (Car tour 2): the Montañas del Fuego ('Fire Mountains') create a unique landscape, rich in volcanic hues and textures. In order to preserve the beauty of this national park, tourists are not allowed to drive through the area on their own. But the coach tour that takes you through the park is a must for every visitor to Lanzarote.

César Manrique is the man. The cave has been skillfully transformed into a night club, maintaining as much natural décor as possible. Penetrating into the depths of the cave, you come to a large crystal-clear sea-pool. Shiny objects on the floor of the pool catch your eye: they are tiny white blind crabs (*Munidopsis poliforma*), unique to the sea world. You ascend to a large opening in the ground and a swimming pool set in a rock garden (in Jameos del Agua) bursting with colour (see photograph page 20).

Returning to the main road, we cross it and head up to the **Cueva de los Verdes★**, 1km away. The entrance to the cave remains obscure — no ticket office, souvenir shops or stalls scar the place. Thanks to, guess who? Only one of the seven kilometres of this vast complex of tunnels is open to the public. With a guide, you wind down through low, narrow passageways and emerge into enormous cool chambers — one of them an auditorium with perfect acoustics. The Guanches sought refuge in these caves whenever there were pirate raids. The caves were created when streams of molten lava solidified into a tunnel, and the crust outside cooled faster than the internal flow.

Back on the GC710, turn left for Orzola. Following the coast, we run along the edge of Malpais ('Badlands') de la

Jameos del Agua — like the Mirador del Río, one of César Manrique's fine creations.

Corona — an expansive undulating plateau of lava carpeted in a thick mat of greenery. Patches of sand and a couple of sandy coves embraced in the rocky shoreline break up the lava flow. Soon see the table-topped island of Alegranza over to your right — and the north of La Graciosa. Rocky reefs create lagoons along the shoreline, and these are ideal for swimming.

Orzola (53km 🏠✗ and 🛏 to La Graciosa), at present an ordinary fishing village, is all set for a 'face-lift'. The Famara massif rises up into a bold block of hills in the background, standing guard over the little port. Here's where you catch the ferry, if you're planning to do Walk 1 or picnic on La Graciosa.

Now making for the Mirador del Río, we climb inland, still circling the *malpais* on a narrow winding road. A wavy blanket of greenery, pierced by rocky outcrops, stretches below. We rejoin the GC710 at the foot of Montaña Corona — a massive sharp-rimmed crater that dominates the north of the island — and ascend to the right. Thick stone walls soon take over the countryside; their precision transforms the fields into a work of art. An imposing solitary villa, Torrecilla de Domingo, rises up out of this maze of walls, crowning a hilltop in the shadows of Montaña Corona (photograph page 42). We pass above the Quemada crater; Walk 3 circles it.

Shortly the route passes by Ye (where Walk 3 ends), a small farming community cast across a sloping plateau below Corona's gaping crater. Crossing the plateau, you look straight down into deep valleys. In spring the top of the plateau is flecked with poppies, dandelions, daisies and *Echium*. A porthole window set in a stone wall that encloses a carpark is all that gives away the **Mirador del Río ★** (🕮). This well-camouflaged lookout is embedded in the top of the **Risco** (Cliff) **de Famara ★**. From here you look straight out over the Río channel onto the bare and barren — yet strangely beautiful — Graciosa Island, which sits just below. This is a view unequalled on Lanzarote, and one of the best vistas in all the Canaries. The mountain island (Montaña Clara) and Alegranza enhance this already magnificent sea view. The *mirador* balcony hangs out over a precipitous wall plummeting 450m/1475ft below, and you look down onto the landscapes of Walk 2 shown on pages 37 and 38: the exquisite Playa del Risco and the captivating salt pans of El Río Note: the exterior of this setting is worth seeing from the cliff-top above (from where the photograph on page 17 was taken). The *mirador* occupies the site of a 16th-century pirate lookout.

Continuing south, we edge along the cliffs of Famara. This wall of rock stretches for 23km and reaches a height of 600m/1970ft, as it slices its way along the northwest coast The road (one-way, fortunately) is narrow and vertiginous — even on foot! You recapture the very dramatic *mirador* vista a little further on, where you are able to pull over safely. In the distance ahead you see the vast Jable plain stretching inland behind Playa de Famara, and the hills growing up out of the west coast.

Leaving the plateau we overlook a rocky basin of farmland—the other side of Ye. Pass the most stunning picnic spot on the island (*P*2) — also set in these cliffs. Meet a junction at 68km and continue straight on for Haría/Arrecife. Descending to **Máguez** (72km ✕ *P*3), we cross a large declining valley. See the

Car tours 1 and 2: The restaurant at Monumento al Campesino is a beautifully-restored farmhouse.

Montaña Corona, rising off the plateau behind Máguez (Picnic 3)

craters over on your right? Walk 3 (Alternative) circles this very quiet and scenic mound of volcanoes. Máguez is a rambling, pleasantly scruffy country village with a peaceful air about it. Keep right on entering the village … or turn left for the picnic spot.

Over in the next valley lies **Haría** (74km ✗ M), a handsome settlement embellished with palms. This oasis of greenery boasts the largest number of palms in the Canaries. (I wonder what Gomera has to say about this?) Bougainvillea, geraniums, and hibiscus splash the village with colour, and the grand shady plaza adds a touch of class. Keep right through the narrow streets, to continue to Teguise. Exiting this valley of palms we wind up a rocky crest. Some 4km from Haría we pass the Mirador de Haría (◉ ✗). Just beyond the *mirador*, we head below Lanzarote's highest (but barely noticeable) summit — Las Peñas del Chache (670m/2200ft), which houses a miltary installation.

Car tour 2: The green lagoon that sits at the foot of the Golfo crater. Rich volcanic hues and an intense blue sea enhance this splendid setting. See also page 24.

Descending out of the hills we make a 3km side-trip, by turning up a road signposted for Las Nieves (on the right). *Note:* This is the *second* turn-off for Las Nieves that you come to. The Ermita de las Nieves (**P**4) stands in solitude, high on a windswept plateau. The 18th-century chapel (open only on the patron saint's day in September) marks the site where the Virgin appeared to a young shepherd. From the edge of the plateau you have a splendid view down onto the extensive Playa de Famara and over the semi-desert Jable plain. The Risco de Famara topples off to an abrupt end here.

Stone walls fence off the countryside on our approach to Los Valles. The interior of the island opens up, as low-slung valleys peel back and rounded hillocks rise in the background. **Los Valles** (88km) sits on the edge of a sweeping basin patched in huge cultivated squares. Here we find the best examples of the traditional Arcadian houses – low oblong buildings with very few (and very small) windows. Cocks (haystacks) set amidst the houses and farm buildings set off this rural landscape. Beyond Los Valles we cross the basin and bump our way into Teguise. Pass the turn-off to the 16th-century Castillo de Santa Bárbara (■;1.3km up a gravel road). This modest fortress commands a good view over the surrounding countryside from its volcano-edge perch. It was once a watchtower to warn against the raiding Moors.

Teguise★ (95km ✗✢✢M; drawing page 4), the island's ancient capital, is Lanzarote's showplace. The village still retains its original character of cobbled streets, stately old buildings, and spacious plazas. In the main square you'll find the imposing Church of San Miguel and, just off the square, the 18th-century Palacio de Spinola. The convents of Santo Domingo and San Francisco are hidden in amongst the houses.

Leaving the glaring whiteness of Teguise, follow the GC730 as far as the La Caleta/Famara turn-off, 3km out. Now we make for the coast. The dusty fishing village of **La Caleta de Famara** (112km ⬤✗) boasts some fine seafood restaurants. To reach the quieter end of this long black-sand beach, pass through the bare *urbanización* and take the track below the cliffs.

Returning to the GC730, bear right and enter **Mozaga** (126km ✗🖻; see Tour 2). At the intersection here we turn left and head home via **San Bartolomé** (keep right through the village) and **Tías** — the outgoing route for Tour 2.

Car tour 2: Looking across the beach of El Golfo crater, from the lookout point just above the village of El Golfo. You can't see the lagoon from this point; it is illustrated on page 23.

2 TIMANFAYA AND THE SOUTHERN BEACHES

Puerto del Carmen • San Bartolomé • Tinajo • La Santa • Montañas del Fuego • Yaiza • El Golfo • Playa Blanca • Papagayo • Femés • La Geria Valley • San Bartolomé • Puerto del Carmen

150km/93mi; 4 hours driving (plus 1 hour's coach tour in the National Park); Exit B from Puerto del Carmen

En route: *P*6, 7, 8, 9; Walks 5, 6, 7, 8, 9

Roads are generally narrow, bumpy and slow going. Some 16km of road is gravel (at press date). Watch for pedestrians and animals on the roads; both are oblivious to traffic.

Opening hours:

Timanfaya National Park: 09.00-17.00 daily, with coach tours operating from 09.00-16.00 daily
Monumento al Campesino: 10.00-17.00 Mondays to Fridays; 10.00-19.00 Saturdays, Sundays and holidays

---

This southern route allows you plenty of time for short strolls, a swim, and perhaps some wine-tasting — if you make a day of it. Volcanology may not be one of your favourite topics, but this drive will certainly arouse your interest in it. Over the last two and one-half centuries violent eruptions have left a curious landscape in their wake. The National Park bus tour — a must for everyone — immerses you in this moonscape of rich volcanic hues. It will be the highlight of your day, if not of your entire holiday on Lanzarote. More curiosities follow, however. La Geria, the valley of ash, and the home of *malvasia* wine, is another amazing sight. Here the vineyards create a scenery of their own. The eroded Golfo crater, with its dazzling green lagoon, is something akin to an artist's palette, with all its colours and blended hues. And if all this isn't enough, then there are the golden sandy beaches of the southeast, of which Papagayo has become the most popular amongst tourists. You'll soon see why.

Leave Puerto del Carmen on the Tías (5km ✕🚌) road (Exit B, the return route of Tour 1). We bypass Tías, cross straight over the GC720, and wind up over hills into the vast sloping valley overlooked by **San Bartolomé** (11km ✕). Volcanic cones stand above us. Vivid splashes of scarlet poppies, white daisies, and yellow dandelions light up the surrounding farmlands. Head straight through this sprawling village, keep to the right of the main square and, when you reach the GC740, turn left for Tinajo.

At the junction for Mozaga (14km ✕🚌) we're confronted with another of Manrique's works — the Monumento al Campesino ★, dedicated to the island's country dwellers. This bold ultra-modern structure stands

25

in pleasant surroundings, with a restaurant (a beautifully-restored farmhouse; see page 21) that specialises in local dishes, and a small souvenir shop. Passing through the junction, we come into the hamlet of **Mozaga**. The setting is particularly picturesque: the houses are dispersed amidst great blocks of lava, which are brightly speckled with green *Aeoniums*. Neat, fresh-green garden plots border the lava plain.

Tao (17km ✗⚏) occupies a slight rise with a fine view across the sweeping Jable plain to the cliffs of Famara and the islands. A sprinkling of elegant palms complements this pleasant rural setting. We pass through **Tiagua** (18km ✗) in the thick of these gardens.

An avenue of palms leads us into the expansive farming settlement of **Tinajo** (23km ✗⚏), where Walk 5 ends. Entering the village, turn right for La Santa. Descending to the coast, the red Montaña Bermeja catches your eye, rising off the shore below left. The countryside becomes harsher, rough and bumpy with hillocks, and the terrain is strewn with stones. **La Santa** (28km ✗) is a small village of restaurants set back off the shore. The rather exclusive sports complex, Club La Santa (30km ▲▲✗), lies a couple of kilometres further on. It overlooks the rocky islet, La Isleta, and a pretty lagoon. A pleasant interlude in this desolate stretch of coast. To cross the *isleta*, pass the hotel entrance and then keep right.

Returning to Tinajo, keep straight on through the village to **Mancha Blanca** (41km), where we turn off for Montañas del Fuego. Mancha Blanca, starting point for Walk 5, rests on a shelf overlooking its tidy ash fields, on the edge of a sea of lava that floods the southwest. Everything here grows in straight rows, as you can see in the photograph on page 49. The village is the home of the island's female patron saint — Our Lady of the Volcanoes, who is credited with having saved Tinajo from a lava flow. A popular festival celebrates the saint's day on September 15th each year.

When we mount the lava plateau another world awaits us: the world of fire and brimstone, where two centuries ago all hell let loose and (as one witness described it) "the earth suddenly opened up and an enormous mountain rose from the bosom of the earth and from its apex shot flames which continued to burn for 19 days". This catastrophic eruption lasted intermittently for some six years (1730 to 1736), burying one-third of the island (including eleven villages) under metres of lava … an eruption unsurpassed in recorded history. Less than one hundred years later another eruption increased the existing number of volcanoes from 26 to 29.

Crossing this lonely but curiously beautiful landscape is like being on another planet, hence it should come as no surprise to learn that the first astronauts were shown photographs of the national park in preparation for their moon flight. The road cuts its way through rough sharp lava. Lichen flecks the rock, creating the impression of freshly fallen sleet. An assortment of volcanoes with hints of red, clay brown, and deep maroon grow out of the lava.

Large mounds of cinder soon close in on us. Some 9km from Mancha Blanca we turn off for **Islote de Hilario**—the departure point for the coach tours ★. An entrance fee, which includes your coach tour, is paid as you go into the park area. Islote de Hilario is named for a hermit (Hilario) who returned here after the eruptions had subsided to build a hut and plant a fig tree (which, incidentally, is *not* the fig in the restaurant...) — the only tree in the national park. The restaurant here makes good use of the thermal energy — temperatures reaching 360°C only six metres below the surface of the ground. Your excursion bus twists up, down, and around the great volcanoes, affording you stunning views over the park and into the craters of the Montañas del Fuego, which drip with endless blends of colours (see page 19).

Leaving the park and continuing south, we climb and pass alongside the russet-brown slopes of Montaña del Fuego, where the much-publicised camel ride ★ begins (at 56km). You're bound to see a camel train ascending or descending — complete with awkwardly-seated tourists astride the hump-backs. Still, it's an impressive sight, no matter how 'touristic'. Also, take note of the different type of lava formation on the left-hand side of the road here: this lava, with great cracks in its crust, is *pahoehoe* lava (also known as 'ropey lava'; the name is Hawaiian).

Out of the lava fields we come into the charming white-washed village of **Yaiza** (61km ✗▱⊕✝), where Walk 7 begins and ends. Turn right at the junction here. Pass the cool, shady Los Remedios Square. Across from it stands the 18th-century church of the same name. This proud village has some fine old balconied houses, and the gardens overflow with colour. Barely 2km from Yaiza we leave the main south road and fork off right onto a gravel road to make for El Golfo. A traffic island full of geraniums marks the intersection. Bouncing over potholes we re–enter more jagged lava fields; these are interrupted by stony *islotes* (islands of lava-free ground; see photograph page 47). Keep left at the fork just over 4km along.

Meet the road to El Golfo and bear right. Crossing a crest, you descend to **El Golfo** ★ (69km ✕▣), a small seaside village of restaurants. The encompassing dark lava is lit up by bushes of resplendent green *tabaiba*. An unmarked *mirador* just before the village gives you an excellent view (see page 24) over the eroded Golfo crater★. This majestic submarine volcano has been spectacularly eaten away by the sea, leaving one with the impression that it has been sliced in half. The best access to the *golfo*, the crescent-shaped bay, is 2km back along the road. The first fork-off right leads you to a large parking area. Strolling down to the crater, you're greeted by a striking sight: an array of greys, browns, and reds oozes out of the cone and surrounding rock. A strong blue sea and a cloudy green lagoon ★ set at the base of the crater enhance this rainbow of colours, shown on page 23.

Following the coastline further south, we drive through billowing waves of lava. The colourful Montaña Bermeja soon commands your attention with its glowing orange-brown cone. Less than 2km from El Golfo's crater, you'll come to an unsignposted lay-by on your right. From here a path leads off to a *mirador* called Los Hervideros (▣; the 'boiling springs'), where the sea pounds into sea-caves. There's little to see here. However, from another lay-by 200m further along, the sight is made more impressive because the bright cone of Montaña Bermeja stands in the background. The lazy hills of Los Ajaches, leaning one against the other, rise up prominently ahead. Las Breñas is the village you see sprinkled along a raised shelf at the foot of the hills.

Turning inland, we round the salt pans of Janubio (Las Salinas de Janubio; see photograph page 61). They lie cradled in a deep basin off a land-locked lagoon and the curving black sand beach of Janubio. You look down onto a fine mosaic of tiny white squares of drying salt and ponds. The colours of this basin turn the severe countryside into quite a beauty spot, especially in the evening. Entering the hamlet of **La Hoya** — and just before rejoining the main south road — an unsignposted lookout (▣) allows you to pull over and get a few photographs of this interesting sight — the setting for Walk 8.

Head right along the GC720 for Playa Blanca. Some 800m along, a crest jutting out above the lagoon (a

signposted *mirador*, ⏷) enables you to view the *salinas*
from the other side. The turn-off for *Picnic 8* and the beach
(signposted 'Playa') comes up after another 800m. Then,
crossing the featureless, stone-strewn Rubicón plain, we
reach **Playa Blanca** (98km ▲▲♦✕🖙 and 🚢 to
Fuerteventura), a small fishing village swallowed up by a
mass of bungalows, hotels, apartments and all the
paraphernalia of tourism. Fuerteventura sits enticingly
close — just a 40-minute ferry trip away.

The only reason that I would bring you this far south is
to see the unspoilt beaches that hide in the scenic
southeastern coastline. Once in Playa Blanca, bear left
and remain on this road all the way out to Papagayo (6km
away). On the outskirts of Playa Blanca, meet a T-junction
and keep right along a gravel road. For the first few
kilometres you may encounter roadworks. There is a plan
to build a tarred road all the way out to Papagayo. There's
no signposting at present, and tracks branch off in all
directions to the various beaches en route. Stay on the
main track/road, just by following everyone else. You'll
cross a barren stony shelf that lies at the foot of the Ajaches
hills. All the beaches along here are different, and all are
enticing. Just choose amongst them! Before reaching
Papagayo, we branch off left to Playa de Puerto Muelas
(better known to tourists — and signposted — as 'La
Caleta'). This is the unofficial — and, needless to say, very
popular — nudist beach. **Papagayo**, with its few derelict
houses, is the hippy hangout. All the other beaches are for
you and me — perhaps for enjoying *Picnic 9* (photograph
page 64).

Femés, our next destination, *can* be reached via a dusty
gravel road that cuts across the Rubicón (had we taken the
first or second turn-off right immediately outside of Playa
Blanca). But it's more comfortable to go via Las Breñas. So
we return to the junction for El Golfo and turn right.
Keeping left through **Las Breñas**, meet a T-junction and
ascend to the left. A superb panorama over the plain to
Playa Blanca and out to Fuerteventura soon unfolds. You
see the 'pimply' island of Lobos and the white dunes of
Corralejo directly behind it. The hills tower above you,
with ridges tumbling out of them in all directions. The road
zig-zags up to a narrow pass, and just on the saddle sits
Femés (118km ✕⏷), overlooking the flat Rubicón plain.
Your view is framed by the encircling hills. Take a break
and enjoy the vista from this *mirador* — or *Picnic 7*. The
church is dedicated to San Marcial, the island's patron

saint. Femés is a precious little village, set high up in an already elevated valley and shut off from the rest of the island.

Exiting through fields, we drop down out of the valley and back onto the GC720. Cross straight over the main road and join the GC730 just above **Uga** (124km ✕). Uga is a colourful village with a North African flavour about it. It rests in a saucer of gardens with its back up against the dark lava sea of the Timanfaya National Park. Continue straight on at the junction above Uga. Rounding a corner, the scenery changes yet again, as we enter the intriguing valley of La Geria (**P**6, 600m past the junction), a dark sweeping depression, further pitted with hollows. The slopes are coated in black ash. Myriad low half-moon stone walls edge the hollows and stretch across the countryside (see photographs on pages 51 and 53). This is the home of *malvasia* wine, the product of an ingenious farming method: The vines are planted in crater-like depressions layered with *lapilli*, which absorb the moisture from the air and enable a single vine to produce up to as much as 200 kilos of grapes. (Note: the valley road is very narrow here — so hopefully you will not meet any oncoming traffic….)

Leaving La Geria, we re-enter the lava — this time 'ropey' lava, which still has molten lava flowing under its solidified surface. (The ripples and ruptures in the surface are caused by this movement.) Strips of encroaching 'AA' lava, encrusted with lichen, give the effect of stagnant, weed-infested ponds. Cheerful green *Aeoniums* freckle the landscape. **Masdache** (135km ✕) lies amidst this upheaval of lava. Here's your chance to do some wine-tasting, at the *bodega* on the outskirts of the village. But remember: you still have to drive home! A row of prominent, gaping craters lines the landscape on your right. Re-entering vineyards and vegetable gardens, serenity returns to the countryside. A couple of kilometres beyond Masdache, we turn off right for San Bartolomé, where we rejoin this morning's route. Entering San Bartolomé, keep straight on until you reach an intersection, where you will see an avenue of palm trees across from you. Here turn right and continue straight on past the village square, to return to your base at Puerto del Carmen.

1 AROUND LA GRACIOSA

Distance: 19km/11.8mi; 3h15min

Grade: easy, but fairly long. Can be very hot. No shade

Equipment: comfortable shoes, sunhat, light cardigan, raingear, swimwear, suncream, picnic, plenty of water

How to get there: 🚢 from Orzola to La Graciosa departs 10.00 daily; connecting 🚌 from Arrecife departs 08.00 daily

To return: 🚢 from La Graciosa departs 16.00 daily; connecting 🚌 from Orzola departs 17.00 daily

Short walk: from Caleta del Sebo to the tidal lagoon (45min; easy). Heading out from Caleta del Sebo turn off left for the cemetery (see map), which lies 10min up. Then descend to the sea, bearing slightly right. In 7min, you'll reach the lagoon . . . if the tide is in. This is a beautiful spot to spend the day if you don't want to walk far; the return along the seashore takes 25 minutes. Note that there's little shade.

All of you will have seen La Graciosa from the Mirador del Río. The vista is unsurpassed. For many people, this view from the mirador is sufficient. But this little desert island deserves a second chance. Take a ferry over and see for yourself. You'll discover superb beaches, sand dunes, lop-sided craters, and a lagoon. The fishing village, Caleta del Sebo, seems to be in perpetual slumber; a relaxing calm pervades. There are no roads, and thus no traffic. You'll follow tracks by Shanks's pony.

Getting there is fun in itself. Taking the pint-sized ferry over, you pass through the straights of El Río in the shadows of the towering Famara cliffs. (Note: the sea can be choppy!)

Once you've got your legs back on steady ground again — on the quay at Caleta del Sebo, **head off** along the waterfront to the left. The village is a simple fishing haven of small low-slung houses. There are no gardens, no trees. Stark naked! At the end of the promenade, veer inland up past Bar Girasol Playa (which is also a pension). A dusty track takes you up onto a gravel road on your right. Remain on this road.

Out of the houses you cross a sandy/gravelly flat area, covered in various species of salt-resistant vegetation — *Launaea arborescens* (*aulaga*), *Mesembryanthemum nodiflorum* (*cosco*), *barilla* (the 'ice plant'), *Schizogyne sericea* and *Traganum moquinii*. Looking back down the track you have a superb shot over the village clustered along the water's edge to the dramatic Risco de Famara and the striking Playa del Risco (Walk 2), curving round the foot of the cliffs. On windy days you'll curse this dusty terrain. The two volcanoes, Pedro Barba (right) and Montaña del Mojón (left), rise up ahead on either side of the track. A third, Montaña Clara (an island), soon appears in the background, centred between the other two.

Three minutes past a branch to the left the track forks, just in front of the village dump. Go right for Caleta de Pedro Barba. Reddish *cosco* brightens up the inclines. Heading along the base of Montaña Pedro Barba, your view stretches beyond the wall of cliffs to the Jable plain and the distant volcanoes of Timanfaya. Some **40min** from the village cross a low crest and descend onto a lower plain, edged by short, abrupt hills. Alegranza comes into sight, rising up out of the sea into an impressive table-topped mountain trailed by a tail of hills. The remains of rock walls come as a surprise out here. What could they have grown?

At just over **50min** come to a branch-off left — our continuation, which circles the island. But why not first visit the beautifully-kept little port of Caleta de Pedro Barba: stay on the main track and head to the right; it's only seven minutes away. All the fishermen's old cottages there have been given glamorous 'facelifts'. Gardens filled with palms and shrubs encircle them, and a sandy cove sits just below. The good-sized jetty, which encloses a pool, points to the fact that this is no ordinary weekend retreat — it's a lovely serene spot with a good outlook over the cliffs and to Orzola.

Continuing around the island, we head towards Alegranza on a rougher track. The north coast is sandier; dunes grow into the landscape. Ignore the faint forks off to the right within the next ten minutes. *Polycarpaea nivea*, a dense, silvery-leafed plant, grows in the dunes. *Suaeda vera* crowns the little ant hills of sand that cover the plain. Montaña Bermeja (Red Mountain) soon appears on your left, and Montaña Clara reappears, seemingly joined to the island. At about **1h20min** the track forks; keep left and head towards the dunes to make for Playa del Ambar. What appears at first to be a lovely beach soon becomes a disappointment — it's littered with washed-up rubbish. Moreover, the rocks beneath the water's surface make swimming here awkward. The setting, however, makes an appealing photograph — the white dunes, green sea, and the volcanic-coloured mountains in the background. Don't worry — a better beach is en route! *Note:* the west-coast beaches are usually treacherous; take care when swimming!

The track heads around behind and above the beach, fading as it crosses the dunes. Just after dropping down to

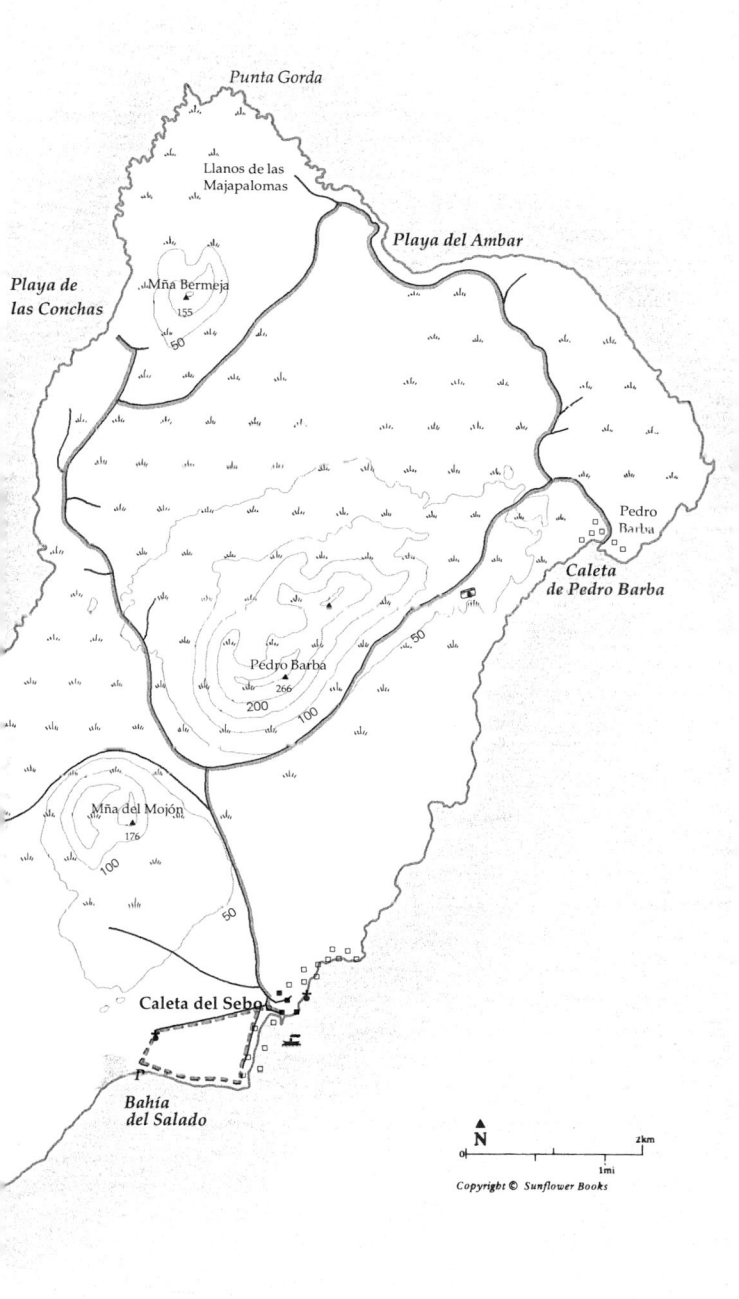

Punta Gorda

Llanos de las
Majapalomas

Playa del Ambar

Playa de
las Conchas

Mña Bermeja
▲
155

50

Pedro
Barba

Caleta
de Pedro Barba

50

Pedro Barba
266
200   ▲

100

Mña del Mojón
176

100

50

Caleta del Sebo

Bahía
del Salado

▲
N

0   2km

1mi

Copyright © Sunflower Books

Playa de las Conchas, at the foot of Montaña Bermeja

the shoreline, a few minutes around the beach, we meet our turn-off, some 30min from the Caleta de Pedro Barba junction. Attention: it's a very faint track striking off left; it quickly becomes more obvious. Don't continue straight on; that way leads to Punta Gorda.

Shortly you're alongside Montaña Bermeja. The dunes lose their strength and flatten out, and Pedro Barba now reveals its crater. Further along, the Timanfaya side of Lanzarote comes into sight. Approaching the coast (**2h05min**), you come to a T-junction (just before a strip of sand dunes). Now an exquisite beach lies only ten minutes along to your right. It rests at the foot of the deep maroon slopes of Montaña Bermeja. This clean beach of golden sands, Playa de las Conchas (see above) drops deeply into a blue sea. Montaña Clara stands up boldly, across the water. This is a prize spot . . . but don't forget to check: how are you doing for time?

A left turn at the T-junction (2h05min) takes you between the two craters and back to Caleta del Sebo. It's a gentle ascent over a low col littered with stones and rocks. Ignore all the branch-offs. Heading between the craters the Risco reappears like a green stage curtain, bringing an end to the walk. At **2h50min** you rejoin the track on which you started out; turn right for the port. All the boat passengers congregate around the Marinero bar/restaurant before the boat leaves. So grab yourself a much-deserved cool beer. You'll spot the bar as you re-enter the village: pass the Pension Enriqueta and turn left.

2 RISCO DE FAMARA

Map page 40; another photograph page 17
Distance: 13.5km/8.3mi; 3h

Grade: very strenuous — a steep, gravelly descent down a cliff face, with a **possibility of vertigo** for inexperienced walkers. The return is a tough ascent of 400m/1315ft — sheer slog! Don't attempt in wet weather. There's no shade en route, so the walk is not advisable on *very* hot days. Only recommended for experienced and fit walkers.

Equipment: walking boots, sunhat, light jacket, raingear, swimwear, suncream, picnic, plenty of water

How to get there: 🚌 to Ye (departs Arrecife) or Máguez (and walk to the starting point; add 45min), or alight at Haría and take a taxi. *To return:* 🚌 from Máguez

This is a truly spectacular walk. You descend into the landscape viewed from the Mirador del Río and slip and slide your way down the sheer Risco (cliff) de Famara. You discover that the captivating beach that sits imbedded in the lava tongue hundreds of metres below you is accessible after all! (The local people will probably hang me when they find out I've revealed this little-known beauty spot to you....) In the early morning and in the evening, this setting is no less than an oil painting. You'll probably want to make this an all-day hike, so *do be* prepared for the lack of shade.

Alight from the Ye bus at the Mirador del Río junction just before Ye. The road here, to your left (descending from the *mirador*) is for south-bound traffic only. **Setting out** by heading up this road, we pass through the outskirts of Ye. The houses are shuttered and many of the plots lie in tired abandon. Low lichen-clad stone walls criss-cross a countryside clothed in fig trees and prickly pear.

Our first turn-off comes up at **5min.** Landmarks: Soon after a roadside house on your right, you'll see a dyke (natural wall of rock) with a stone wall built into it. It's on the left. Two stone buildings, leaning up against the road, stand behind it. Follow the track that turns off immediately before this wall. A stunning panorama slowly unravels, as you near the cliff-tops a few minutes along. You look straight out on to the stark sandy island of Graciosa (Walk 1), bare of vegetation, desolate, and yet quite beautiful in the eyes of many beholders.... The fishing village of Caleta del Sebo nestles around the exposed shoreline, its small white houses staring up at you. Montaña Clara is the blade of rock that bursts up out of the sea behind La Graciosa and, further afield, to the right, lies the hilly island of Alegranza.

When the track ends continue straight on, now

35

descending on a rocky path. Standing on the very edge of the cliff, you look along a sheer wall of rock that plummets to a flat shelf below. Playa del Risco steals your attention with its golden sand and shallow turquoise-green water. Another sight distracts you: the strangely-coloured pink and maroon (and sometimes orange) ponds of the abandoned salt pans of the Salinas del Río.

One wonders where the path goes from here! It swings down to the right of the power pylon. The view is captivating to say the least; however this path *requires your utmost attention!* No stretches of it are really vertiginous, but you zig-zag straight down. All forks rejoin, so don't worry about deviations. An astonishing amount of plant life clings to these cliffs (see photograph page 17), which harbour the richest source of plant life on Lanzarote. A number of very rare species, as well as nearly all the island's endemic plants are found in this northern massif. In and around these *riscos* you can find *Pulicaria canariensis, Asteriscus schultzii, Reichardia, Kickxia, Aichryson tortuosum,* two species of *Aeonium, Limoniums,* the rare *Echium decaisnei,* a yellow-flowering *Argyranthemum,* and many different grasses.

The desert-like Jable plain and the assortment of volcanic cones that constitute the Timanfaya National Park soon become visible over to the left. Approaching the faint track that cuts across the sea-flat below, you meet a fork. The right-hand branch is clearer, and in thirty minutes from the top of the cliff it takes you to the track. Turn right along it. Looking back up the way you came, you're bound to be impressed. Moreover, you know that at least here you *can* escape the press of tourists.... Five minutes along, clamber across a dry, gouged-out stream-bed and, five minutes later, the track passes through a stone wall. Some 100m/yds before the wall, you'll spot a faint path descending the side of the bank to reach the beach (**50min**).

Nirvana! At last you can fling off your clothes (hoping that the periscope at the Mirador del Río isn't trained on you ...) and plunge into the cool sea. *Note:* Watch out for broken glass on the beach. Now, whether you decide to swim first or explore the salt pans, your continuation is along this lovely stretch of beach. La Graciosa is just across the straight — almost within swimming distance. At the end of the beach, scramble over the stones and rejoin your track, following it to its end (by an electricity transformer station). The cliffs stand before you — a

The Salinas del Río are one of Lanzarote's undiscovered — and not easily accessible — sights. See also page 38.

formidable barrier of rock. See if you can locate the *mirador* in the cliffs above: this will show you just how well it fits in with its surroundings.

From the track make your way over to the salt pans, again watching out for broken glass. Pass the remains of a derelict building. Towards the end of the pans (*salinas*) you come to the second 'sight' of the walk: a magnificent pink, milk-of-magnesia-coloured pond enclosed by crumbling stone walls (see above). On a fine day you have a clear reflection of the *Risco* in it. On occasions the pools of the shallower pond reached before this one glow a brilliant orange (see page 38).

We return by crossing a footwalk that circles the pink ponds, cutting across the salt pan. Rejoin the track some ten minutes back, then keep left along it. When it fades out a few minutes on, veer uphill to your left — you'll find it becomes clear again. Turn right at a T-junction and remain on the track until your ascending point, barely fifteen minutes along. Relocating the return path requires a keen eye. Four minutes beyond the gouged-out streambed and 100m/yds past a small watercourse (which you cross), you'll see a small pile of stones on your left, marking the ascending point. The ascent is now straightforward. A little over thirty minutes off the track you reach the power pylon. From here we head south on an old path that hugs the edge of the cliff, and we can take in the last of this memorable view. (This stretch of path might prove unnerving for some walkers.) You scale the side of a ridge running parallel to the old washed-out route to the salt pans. Soon come on to a track; follow it up over the crest. Remain on the main track, ignoring all branch-offs.

Descending now, two craters — one stepped above the other — dominate the Guinate Valley below you. The village of Guinate occupies a quiet cultivated corner. Around twenty minutes from the power pylon you exit onto the main road and descend to Máguez (right). The *plaza*/bus stop lies twenty-five minutes downhill.

The Salinas del Río

Distance: 9.5km/6mi; 1h45min

Grade: moderate, with a steady 30-minute climb at the end of the walk. Can be cold and misty.

Equipment: comfortable shoes, jacket, sunhat, raingear, suncream, picnic, plenty of water

How to get there: 🚌 to Máguez (departs from Arrecife)

To return: 🚌 from Ye (*reconfirm departure time before setting out!*), or walk back to Máguez for the bus (add 1h), or telephone the Haría taxi (tel: 83 50 31).

Alternative walk: Máguez—Guinate—Máguez (1h40min; fairly strenuous — with a steep 45-minute ascent at the start — but short). Head straight uphill from the bus stop, following the Mirador del Río sign. Five minutes up, just beyond the second junction, fork off left up a narrow lane into the houses. Metres up the way becomes a track. You remain on this track all the way to Guinate, where the track ends — 100m/yds up from the main north road. A turn-off to the right, some 20min into the walk, heads over into a crater (the site of a small tip) four minutes away. The crater walls harbour an interesting collection of flora. From the top of the plateau, midway along the walk, you have a magnificent view out over the islands. When you reach the main road, bear right for Máguez, 20min away. The bus leaves from the village plaza at the intersection.

O n this pleasant countryside ramble we wind our way amidst the hills of the Famara massif — the highest and (in winter) the most lush corner of the island. Farm plots keep us company. Masses of solid stone walls fortify the inclines. In spring the herbaceous slopes are flecked with dandelions, indigo *Echium*, gold-coloured *Asteriscus*, white *Argyranthemum*, and mauve and scarlet poppies. A splendid sight! The massive yawning craters of Montaña Corona and La Quemada, and the neighbouring Malpais (badlands) de la Corona remind us of the volcanic origins of Lanzarote.

Our walk begins at the small plaza where the bus stops, at an intersection. Follow the road diagonally across from you, the one that heads straight into the village. A minute along pass the colourful church square. Two minutes later, just beyond a large garden plot, we reach an intersection. Turn up left. Ascending (keep straight up) you look back over the village, spread along a gentle valley sprinkled with palms. Just over **5min** up, a road joins you from the right. A minute later, branch off right onto a farm track lined with palms. You exit through hills into another valley. Keep left at the fork a few minutes along, crossing a saucer-shaped valley dominated by the enormous crater of Montaña Corona (609m/1995ft; photograph page 22). A rough patchwork of cultivated fields stretches across the sloping inclines. Just over **20min** from

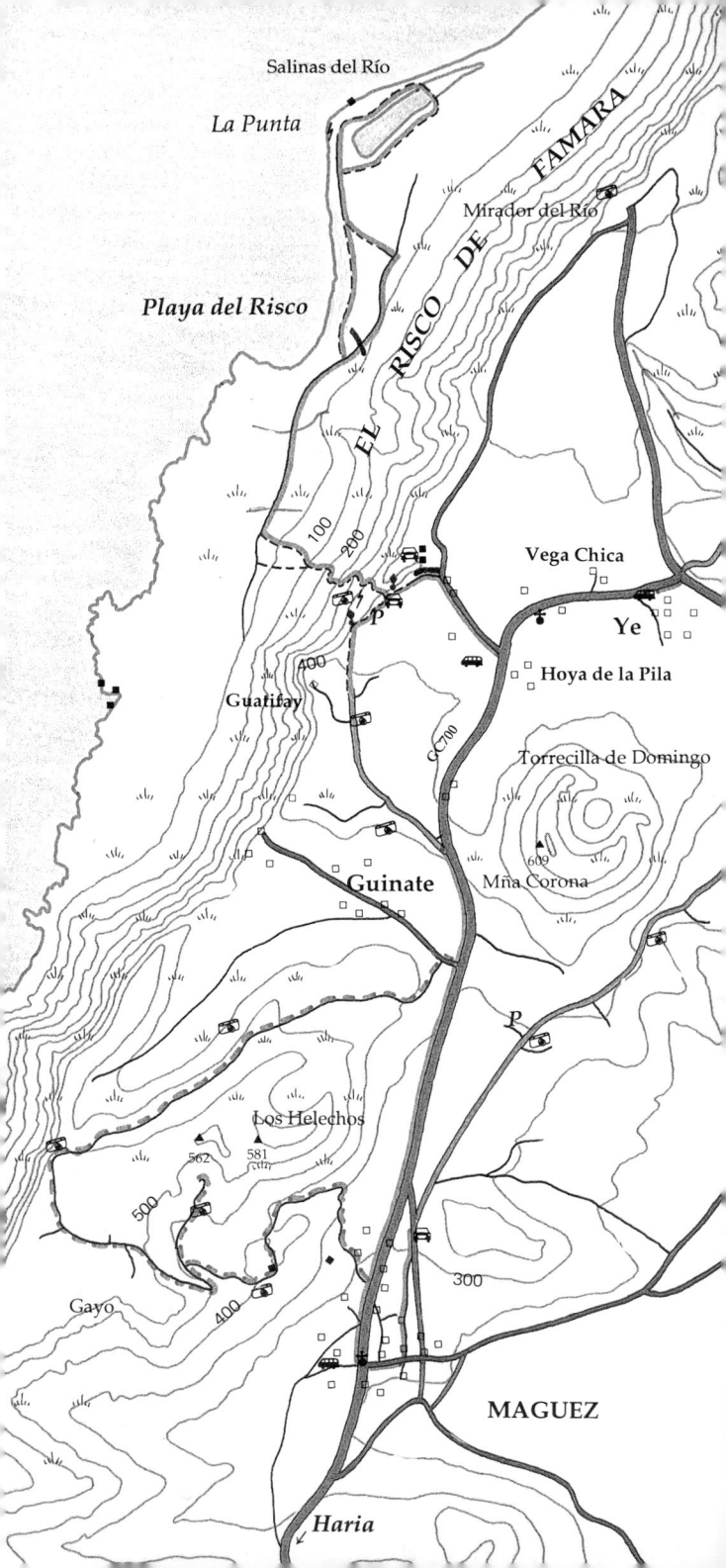

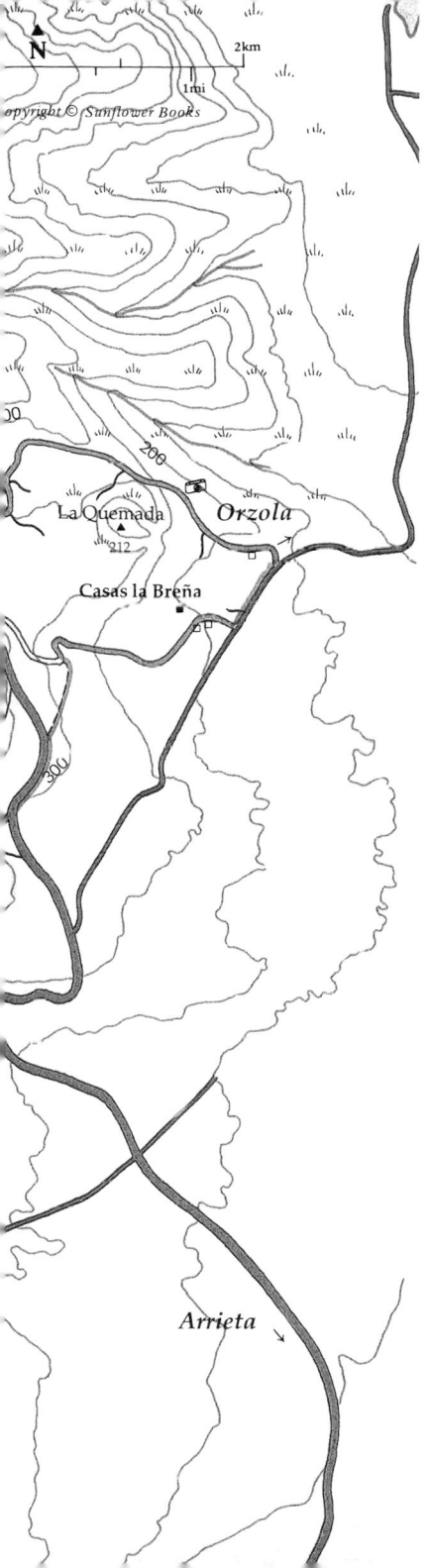

Máguez) we cross an intersection, and then pass two tracks forking off right. Rounding Montaña Corona, the palacial villa, Torrecilla de Domingo (see page 42), captures our attention. It sits high atop a ridge overlooking the northeastern inclines and the sea. On the slopes of Corona you see a plethora of colourful vegetation. But all colour drains out of the landscape, as we approach ash-covered fields and a vast labyrinth of stone walls. Off the hillside, we pass a branch-off to the right and enter this labyrinth.

Close to the Mirador del Río road, at around **40min** into the walk, the track forks. Bear left. On reaching the road, bear left again. A gap in the crater walls above gives you a good view of its sharp-toothed crown and an uninterrupted vista over the spiky interior of Malpais de la Corona. Five minutes up the road a wide mule track flanked by high stone walls veers off to your right and descends towards the *malpais*. A track curves round in front of you five minutes later. Follow it downhill. Our route now circles another extinct volcano (La Quemada), which soon reveals a quite substantial crater. Looking back up the hillside you get a dramatic shot of Montaña Corona: its razor-sharp rim rears up above the wall-rutted slopes.

At **1h05min** exit onto the Orzola road. Turning left along the road, we continue along the edge of the *mal-*

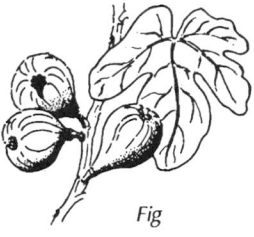

Fig

pais. Some five minutes down the road, turn off onto a track that climbs steeply to your left, circling La Quemada. A steady — and, in stretches, steep — climb takes us up to Ye. Pass a branch-off left. You sidle up against the mountain and get a glimpse of the inside of the crater.

A little over fifteen minutes off the road come to a junction. Keep straight on — right. A deep valley slicing back into the plateau comes out of hiding. Our route dips down and crosses it. Ignore the smaller side tracks. At **1h30min** we ascend into another, higher valley, just below the plateau and come into Ye. This small village sits with its back to the gaping crater of Montaña Corona. Cross the road (to the Mirador del Río) and pick up the road heading into the village centre, to your right. The bus stop lies a couple of minutes along, just beside the public phone box.

The palacial villa of Torrecilla de Domingo against the backdrop of Montaña Corona (Car tour 1; Walk 3)

4 MALA • PRESA DE MALA • ERMITA DE LAS NIEVES • TEGUISE

Distance: 18.5km/11.5mi; 3h

Grade: quite strenuous, with a drawn-out ascent of 608m/1995ft lasting 1h45min. Can be quite cold, windy and misty … or even wet!

Equipment: comfortable shoes, warm jacket, sunhat, raingear, suncream, picnic, plenty of water

How to get there: Máguez-🚌 to Mala (departs Arrecife)
To return: 🚌 from Teguise

Short walks: both are easy. Take private transport to start out; return by bus.
1 Ermita de las Nieves to Teguise (1h10min). Pick up the main walk at the chapel (Ermita de las Nieves) and follow it to the end.
2 Ermita de las Nieves to Mala (1h50min). Again, pick up the main walk at the chapel. Use the map to do the first half of the main walk in reverse; it's very straightforward — but see above notes on weather conditions.

Crossing the island from east to west, we climb to the solitary Chapel of the Snows (Ermita de las Nieves) — the coldest point on Lanzarote. So if you're after some bracing air … join us and leave the sea plain! We wind up into a narrow concealed valley. The denuded clay-brown slopes soon fold up into pasture-like inclines (in winter). Seascapes and mountain views accompany us all the way up to the chapel — where from a windswept plateau we enjoy a 360° panorama — the view of views.

When you leave the bus at Mala (at the *second* stop, beside a telephone cabin), **start by** heading north along the road. Three minutes along, turn off up a road branching off left — the second one you come to, just past a line of palms and mimosas. Immediately in, the road forks. Bear right. Pass the church two minutes up. The village is immersed in fields of prickly pear. You can see the wall of the Presa (reservoir) de Mala ahead, wedged across the mouth of the Valle del Palomo.

Less than **10min** along come to an intersection. The road swings left; we continue straight ahead on a rough track. Our climb begins as we leave the farmland behind. Just before crossing the crest into the Valle del Palomo, we get a good view along the sea plain of Mala, buried under a dark green cloak of prickly pear, and then the carpet of tightly-woven gardens extending back to Guatiza. Close on **20min** up, pass a fork off to the right (to an abandoned building). To see the fish pond-sized reservoir— the only one on Lanzarote —, leave the track and cross the top of the crest; it's only two minutes over the top.

At the **40min**-mark we pass behind some houses and continue climbing. We cross the bed of the stream, and

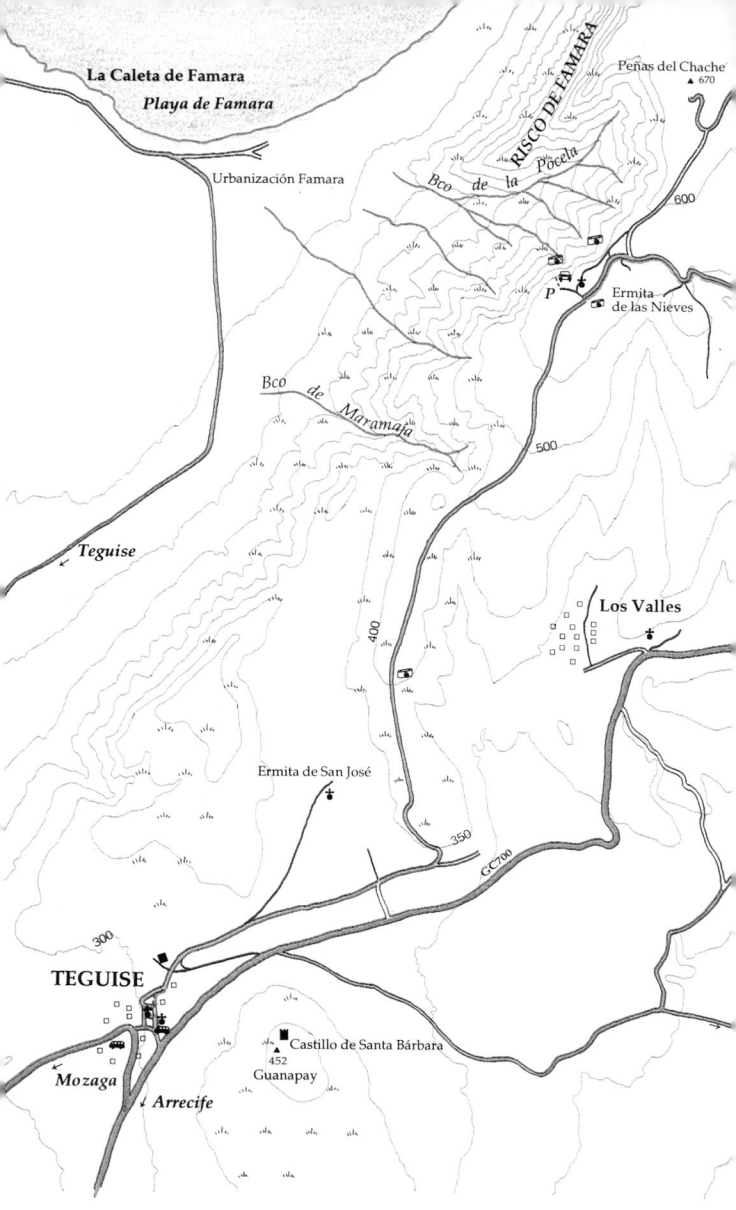

before us see a luxuriantly green valley. After the rains have fallen, this is the most luxuriant valley on Lanzarote. We recross the bed of the *barranco* and the track lazily zig-zags up out of the valley. Yellow, violet and scarlet flowers set the hillside alight. Catch a corner of Malpais de la Corona (Walk 3) over the hills. Mounting the plateau, you swing up past a Lilliputian farm dwelling leaning against a rocky nodule. Two dogs, 'Black' and 'White'(I've so christened them), will come tearing out — barking

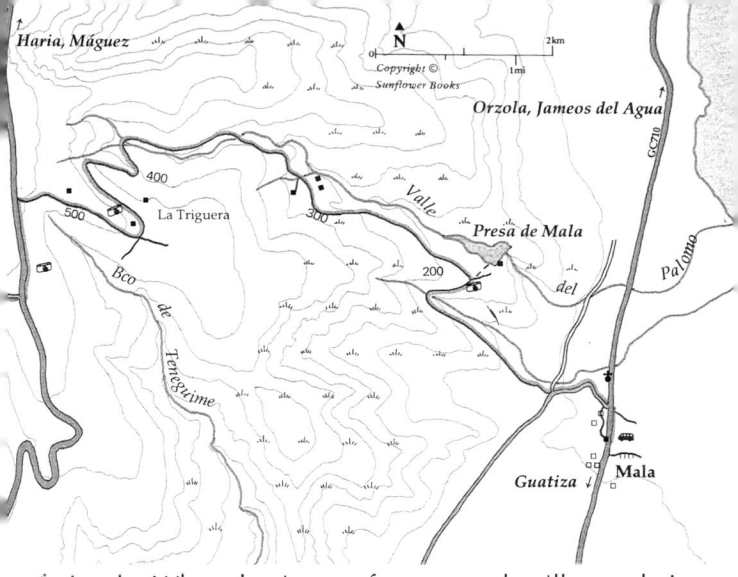

Haria, Máguez

Orzola, Jameos del Agua

Copyright ©
Sunflower Books

400

500   La Triguera   300

Valle

Presa de Mala

Bco   200   del

de

Tenezime   Pa

Guatiza ↓   Mala

furiously. When they're ten feet away, they'll wag their tails and then jump all over you. Black and White keep you company until you reach the main road.

A minute beyond the farmhouse you circle an uninhabited house, and looking back, you have a fine view down onto Arrieta and the sea. To the northwest you see the plateau of Guatifay and the prominent cones of Corona and La Quemada. The great gap separating us from these craters is created by the valleys of Máguez and Haría — an impressive sight. Approaching **1h30min** you exit onto the GC700, bid farewell to Black and White, and head along to your left. Over to the right rises the island's highest summit, Las Peñas del Chache, crowned by a large military installation. As you descend, Llanos de Zonzamos (the sweeping plain behind Arrecife) comes into view, with Arrecife in the background. The refuge of Las Nieves soon captures your attention. It stands conspicuously alone on the *mesa*. Within ten minutes you reach the signposted turn-off to it. Los Valles is visible through the mouth of the *barranco* below. Soon the roar of the sea is heard, and a roadside *mirador* gives you a view over the Playa de Famara far below.

At **1h50min** you're alongside the chapel and probably getting a good battering from the wind. If this is the case, picnic inside the walls that enclose this peaceful haven. For an unparalleled vista head over the cliffs (*carefully*). Below you lies the beach of Famara and, beyond it, the desert-like Jable plain fans inland, littered with remnants of volcanoes. On our right, the Risco de Famara (Walk 2) ends abruptly in a razor-sharp tail; beyond lie the islands of La Graciosa (Walk 1), Montaña Clara and Alegranza.

Once you've soaked up this great view, continue out on the gravel road that descends south of the chapel. It follows the crest of this declining ridge towards Teguise. The local people use this road, and the odd tourist or two will bounce past in a jeep. Shortly the modest Castillo de Santa Bárbara becomes a prominent landmark. Fastened to the crater rim of Montaña Guanapay, it stands guard over Teguise and the encompassing plains. Heading back into fields you descend to an intersection, just over **2h35min** en route (having passed a track joining from the left beforehand). Here the main track turns left to join the GC700; however we keep straight on through the intersection. Ten minutes beyond the intersection, come to a wide track. Bear left along it.

Entering the rear of Teguise, pass the stadium and join a confusion of tracks. Keep straight on, aiming for the church tower. A street leads you down through houses and over a small bridge. Immediately beyond it, leave the street and cross an open space to the church. An arched portal lets you through into a pretty plaza. Exit alongside the Caja de Canarias. Take a peep inside this excellently-restored building. You come out to another beautiful square; here, outside a second church, catch your bus.

The Lilliputian dwelling where 'Black' and 'White' live. We've zig-zagged up out of the Valle del Palomo and now overlook Arrieta and the sea (1h30min into the walk).

5 MANCHA BLANCA • PLAYA DE LA MADERA • TINAJO

Distance: 25.5km/15-3/4mi; 3h30min

Grade: easy but long. Since there is no shade en route, this walk is not recommended in very hot weather. *Note also:* If you plan to swim in the rock pools or at the beach, make *absolutely certain* that the sea is safe. I have never swum at the beach myself, because it never looked safe enough to me!

Equipment: comfortable shoes, cardigan, sunhat, raingear, suncream, swimwear, picnic, plenty of water

How to get there: Tinajo-🚌 to Mancha Blanca (departs from Arrecife)
To return: 🚌 from Tinajo (or taxi)

T his walk will not appeal to everyone. It takes you straight through the vast lava flows that have buried much of the southwest of Lanzarote. Not a soul lives out here — not even plants survive. It's a no-man's land. Deep in its midst, you stumble upon sunken islands of stony lava-free ground, called *islotes* (see below). Here you'll find some plant life and cultivation taking refuge. It's a curious landscape that few would dare to call beautiful, but it has a special allure.

Alight from your bus in Mancha Blanca at the Yaiza— Montana del Fuego junction, and **set off** for Montaña del Fuego. Keep right when the road forks a minute downhill. We skirt this well-dispersed rural village. Stone walls hedge in the road and cordon off the countryside. Here we're on the edge of a sea of 'AA' lava (a sharp, unevenly-surfaced lava; see also Walk 3). The grand crater which dominates the scene is Montaña Blanca (see page 49), and a pint-sized off-sider sits in front of it.

Islotes — tiny oases of greenery (chiefly tabaiba) — light up the dark and inhospitable lava landscape that we explore on Walk 5.

At the T-junction less than **10min** along, head right. From here we follow tarred country lanes through fields. Five minutes later, head left (at the first turn-off). The sharp colour contrast of vivid green plots and ash-grey *lapilli* enhances this picturesque countryside. Montaña de Tenezar rises up boldly at the end of the road. Another junction awaits you at the foot of the mountain, **35min** into the walk. Turn left and continue on a gravel road. You head into lava that now takes over the landscape. Pass two forks off to the right. The craters of Montaña Blanca and son soon bulge up out of the lava. Up close, the mountain's rocky exterior resembles a freshly-baked cake.

Slowly, the off-shore islands appear: Alegranza, the furthest afield, Montaña Clara, and finally La Graciosa (Walk 1). The dark lava drops off into a deep blue sea. Without warning, suddenly the lava flow subsides and reveals a basin of low stony hillocks that lean up against Montaña Blanca like cushions. A couple of stone *casitas* can be seen, set in a coomb in the shoulders of the crater. This is Casas del Islote. We pass the fork-off left to Casas del Islote and Montaña del Fuego at about **1h10min** and dip down into an *islote*.

Some fifteen minutes further on pass another turn-off to the right. From a rise five minutes further on, you spot the first of the beaches, Playa de las Malvas. These black sand beaches are small and the waters usually turbulent. A tiny lagoon sits back off the beach here. Beyond this *playa* we head back into the lava again and, less than ten minutes

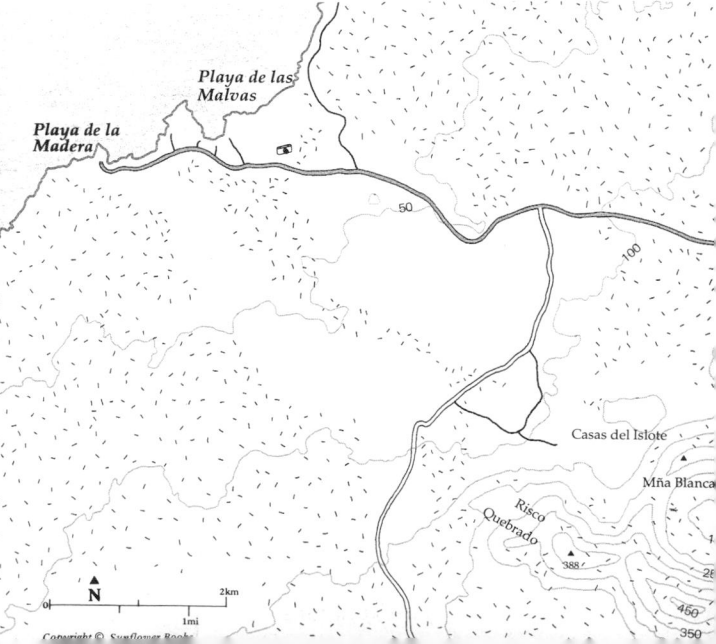

The dark picon-covered gardens of Mancha Blanca, with the yawning crater of Montaña Blanca in the background (Car tour 2, Walk 5)

later, we drop down onto Playa de la Madera. This small cove doesn't look too friendly either. Play it safe and stick to the rock pools. Pillows of yellow-tipped *Zygophyllum fontanesii* (*uvilla* — 'little grapes') grow out of the sand. A path crosses the beach and climbs into the rock on the other side, where stone-built shelters provide good wind-breaks. Shallow and inviting rock pools (*only safe when the sea is calm*) lie beyond the shelters.

Some 1h10min into the straightforward return walk you rejoin the road at the Tinajo—Mancha Blanca junction. This time, keep straight on for Tinajo. La Graciosa is at last in full view, and the Risco de Famara (Walk 2) dramatises the landscape as it bursts straight up out of the sea. Tinajo is a sprinkling of hamlets that sprawls over a large cultivated plain. Entering the village, keep straight along (to the left), passing all turn-offs to the right. On reaching a large intersection, bear left, taking the second of the two roads leading down to the plaza, 1h40min from the beach (**3h30min**). The bus leaves from outside the *dulcería* (cake shop), across from the plaza.

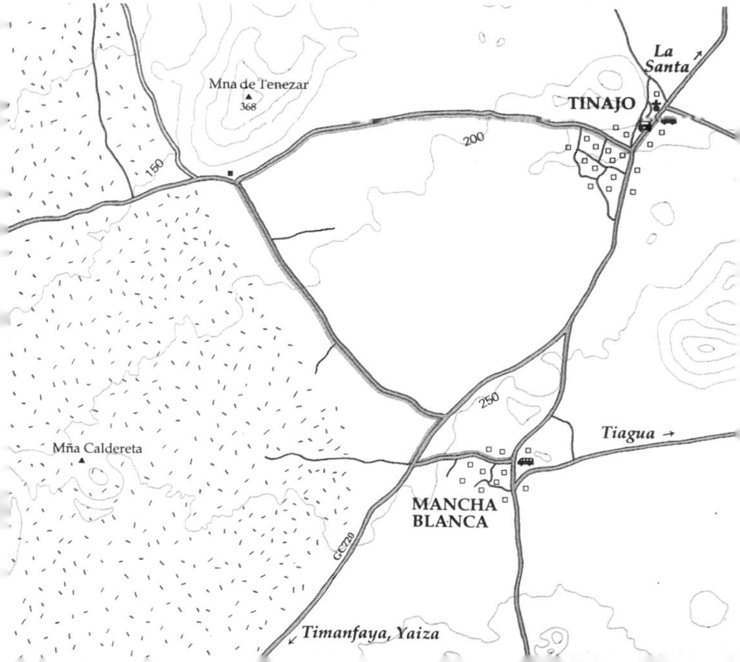

6 UGA • MONTAÑA GUARDILAMA • LA MONTAÑETA • MACHER • PUERTO DEL CARMEN

Distance: 12.5km/7.8mi; 2h15min

Grade: relatively easy, if the mountain ascent is excluded. The ascent of Guardilama involves a steep climb of 160m/525ft, sometimes over loose stones. Be careful on the descent. The climb is also to be avoided in hot weather, but remember, too, that the peak can be very cold and windy!

Equipment: walking boots, jacket, sunhat, suncream, raingear, picnic, plenty of water

How to get there: Playa Blanca-🚐 to Uga (departures from Arrecife and Puerto del Carmen)

To return: 🚐 from Puerto del Carmen

Short walk: Simply exclude the mountain ascent; this takes 25 minutes off the total time and makes for an easy hike. Comfortable shoes are sufficient.

The island's farming methods are of much interest on Lanzarote. With great ingenuity the islanders have been able to grow a variety of produce. This hike takes you through the dark ash fields of La Geria — an intriguing landscape patterned by hollows and stone walls. You then cross the grassy summits that divide east and west, two quite different worlds! Here you'll see the wonders the country folk have worked with the land, and if you speak a little Spanish, they'll be only too proud to show you the way they've gone about it. The *mirador* atop Montaña Guardilama shows you a world of vivid contrasts: vineyards and vegetable plots, meadows and ash fields, and the great lava flows. It opens up the interior of the island for you, and you have a fine outlook over the lunar landscape of the Timanfaya National Park.

Leave the bus outside the church in Uga. **Start out** from the bright and cheerful square here, by heading back the way you came in. Pass a restaurant and come to a junction. Swinging up left, you reach another junction a minute along. Here head left, above garden plots. Two minutes along leave the road and climb a farm track, the first one you come to. You strike off to the right. The route overlooks the village, which nestles in a shallow depression of gardens, its back to a vast expanse of crusty lava. Out of the lava rise the great fire mountains of Timanfaya, their inclines splashed with rust browns and reds. A cluster of adjoining hills stands to the south of the village. These climb into the southern massif — Los Ajaches.

The track carries us up to the Teguise road. A couple of minutes along it, to the left, we fork off right onto another track heading into the hills above. We're now entering the Geria Valley. Vines and fig trees fill the small hollows. The ash fields are ornamented by an assortment of stone walls. Our route takes us straight over the *cumbre*, the island's spine. Ignore all turn-offs. Wandering through this blackened world is quite extraordinary. Over to the left,

From the summit of Montaña Guardilama, we look across the Geria Valley to the volcanoes of Timanfaya. Myriad 'half-moon' stone walls protect grape vines in the crater below (see also page 53).

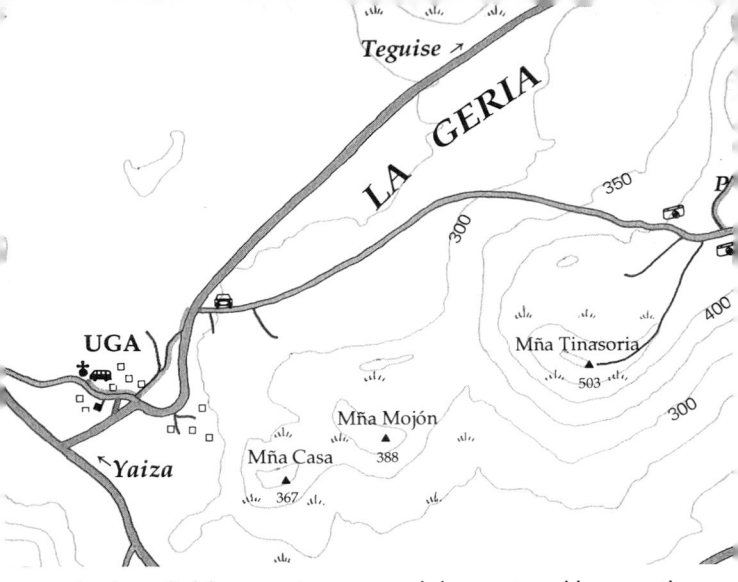

the lava fields grow into a vast lake ruptured by weather-worn cones, and above you stands a line of grass-capped hills that glow with greenery. The solitary white farmsteads stand out like sanctuaries in this inhospitable landscape. Before long, walls take over the countryside. You're entering the vineyards, and the inclines are pock-marked with depressions that are collared by half-circles of stone walls (see page 51 and opposite). We're in malmsey territory, where the well-known *malvasía* origi-nates. This myriad of walls could be the ruins of a grand ancient city.

Crossing the saddle of the *cumbre* the way eases out. You'll have a superb view back over La Geria and Timanfaya. Just over the pass, we turn off for the ascent of Montaña Guardilama, at **40min** into the walk. We follow a faint track that cuts off to the left a few metres beyond the last vineyard (some 150m/yds beyond the second branch-off to the right). Cross a grassy field, briefly running alongside the vineyards, then head straight up the mountain in front of you. When the track ends, continue straight up to the summit — a tiring climb, as it's *very* steep. Nearing the end of the climb, you're scrambling over loose rocks and stones, and this makes the descent quite difficult; *take care!* At the **55min**-mark you flop down on the summit. If it's a windy day, you won't be able to stand upright or even take photos up here! The panorama is, however, magnificent and encompasses the waves of hills in the south, as well as the Risco de Famara and La Graciosa and its neighbouring islets in the north. The sharp rocky crest drops straight down into a cultivated

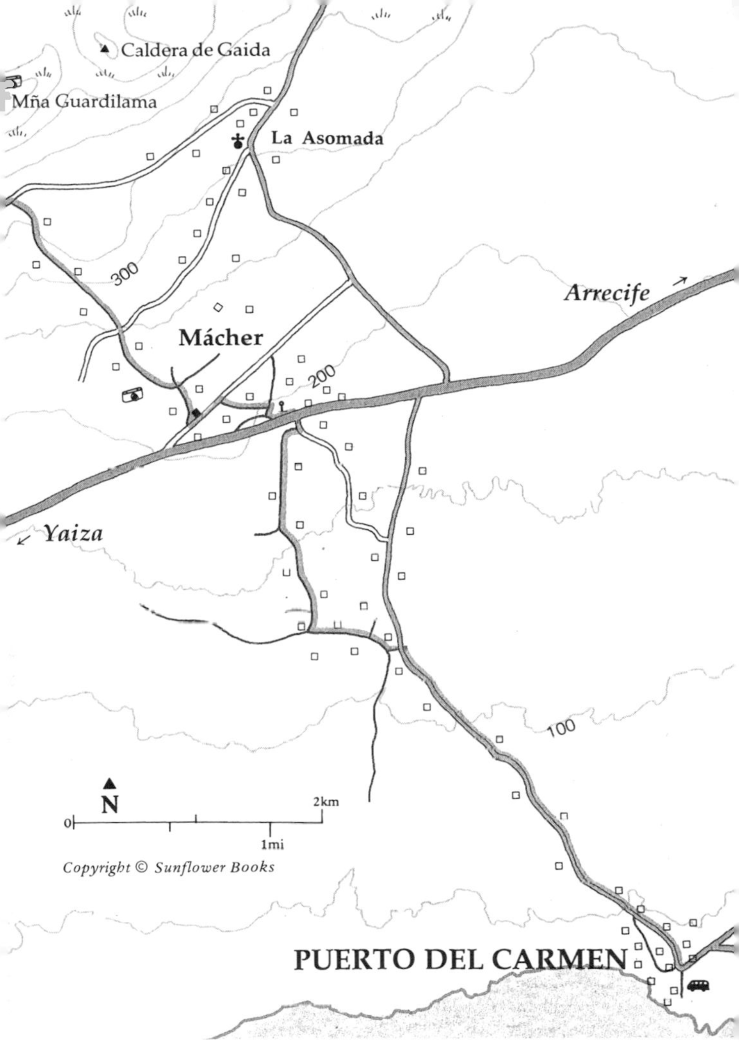

Map

- ▲ Caldera de Gaida
- Mña Guardilama
- ☩ La Asomada
- 300
- **Mácher**
- 200
- ← Yaiza
- Arrecife →
- 100
- **PUERTO DEL CARMEN**

▲
N
0 ———— 1mi ———— 2km

Copyright © Sunflower Books

crater and out onto the pitted ash fields of La Geria (see photograph page 51). Uga and Yaiza lie to the southeast.

Descend slowly and carefully to the main track, where we bear left towards La Asomada. Three minutes along, we fork off the main

A closer view of the half-moon walls protecting malvasia vines in La Geria Valley (see also page 51).

track and descend another to the right. Dropping through plots, come to an intersection (within 10 minutes) and head straight through it. Pass two turn-offs left and, two minutes later, exit onto a road (**1h25min**). Notice the charming old house at the corner here.

Continue up the road to the left, and in two minutes branch off on a small track that heads down to the GC720 just below. When you reach it, cross it and, one minute along to the left, turn off onto a narrow road striking off right. A well-preserved windmill stands above the main road here. Immediately into the turn-off, veer right onto a track. Remain on this track for the next ten minutes, keeping straight down. At the T-junction at the bottom of the track bear left. Five minutes later, just after rounding a corner, you branch left again (the second left), to join the Puerto del Carmen road. The town lies 20 minutes downhill. If you're Arrecife-bound, keep left at the intersection inside the town, and one minute up find your bus stop.

Montaña Guardilama, seen from where our ascent begins. In springtime the slopes are speckled with wild flowers. Enjoy Picnic 6 at the foot of this inviting mountain, or make the steep climb, to enjoy the views shown on page 51.

7 YAIZA • ATALAYA DE FEMÉS • YAIZA

Distance: 10km/6.2mi; 2h45min

Grade: fairly strenuous, with a steady 425m/1435ft ascent. Can be cold and windy.

Equipment: comfortable shoes, jacket, sunhat, raingear, suncream, picnic, plenty of water

How to get there: Playa Blanca-🚌 to Yaiza (departures from Arrecife and Puerto del Carmen)

To return: 🚌 from Yaiza

Short walk: Femés—Atalaya de Femés—Femés (1h; a strenuous, but short, ascent). Accessible by private transport only.

The view from the Atalaya de Femés is best appreciated at sunrise and sunset, when the shadows creep across the countryside, and the last (or first) light captures the real beauty of both Timanfaya and the Salinas de Janubio. Sitting high above the picturesque hamlet of Femés, you have the southern vista of Lanzarote all to yourself. On your ascent you'll often see camels grazing in one of the adjoining valleys. Nearer the summit, goats and a few sheep keep you company.

The bus drops you just before the square. The bleached-white village of Yaiza has won a number of awards for its appearance. It really is picture postcard-perfect, with its resplendent *bougainvillea* and graceful palms. We **start off** by taking the road that turns off left and heads up between the church and the square to a large parking area (from where it continues on to La Degollada). A couple of minutes out we come to a junction. Take the track off to the left, cutting across the valley floor. You look up into a tapering valley and see the hamlet of La Degollada ensconced at the end of it. Halfway across the valley floor you pass through an intersection and continue on a farm track. Ascending the valley wall, pass a faint fork-off left. Mount the crest just over **15min** from Yaiza. A track joins from the left; we continue up this plump ridge, which carries us all the way to the Atalaya de Femés. In the valley over on your left you may see camels.

As you climb, the island opens up, revealing a variety of scenery. Yaiza is in full view below, its brightness accentuated by the intense green garden plots and the dark sea of lava. A barrier of volcanoes, one running onto the next, fills in the backdrop. The track divides, both forks briefly running parallel — keep to the right-hand fork. Come to a fork just over five minutes up the ridge and bear right. Your view becomes more expansive and more rewarding — dipping down now onto Uga and stretching all the way up the dark, shadowy Geria Valley (Walk 6).

At about **30min** the track forks off into three different directions. Yours is the furthest to the right. Mounting another step in the ridge, we see over the sloping plains of the east to Puerto del Carmen and Arrecife. Looking north, notice the line of three lopsided craters. The way dips briefly before reascending, and you're given an introductory glimpse of the Femés Valley. Montaña de Timanfaya, the king of the volcanoes, dominates the National Park, with its distinct reddish-brown slopes.

The way fades as it remounts the top of the crest, which in turn narrows into a sheer-sided 'neck'. Another striking sight follows: the off-white salt pans and the khaki-green lagoon of the Salinas del Janubio shimmering in the sun. Scaling the final head of hills, the track briefly disappears,

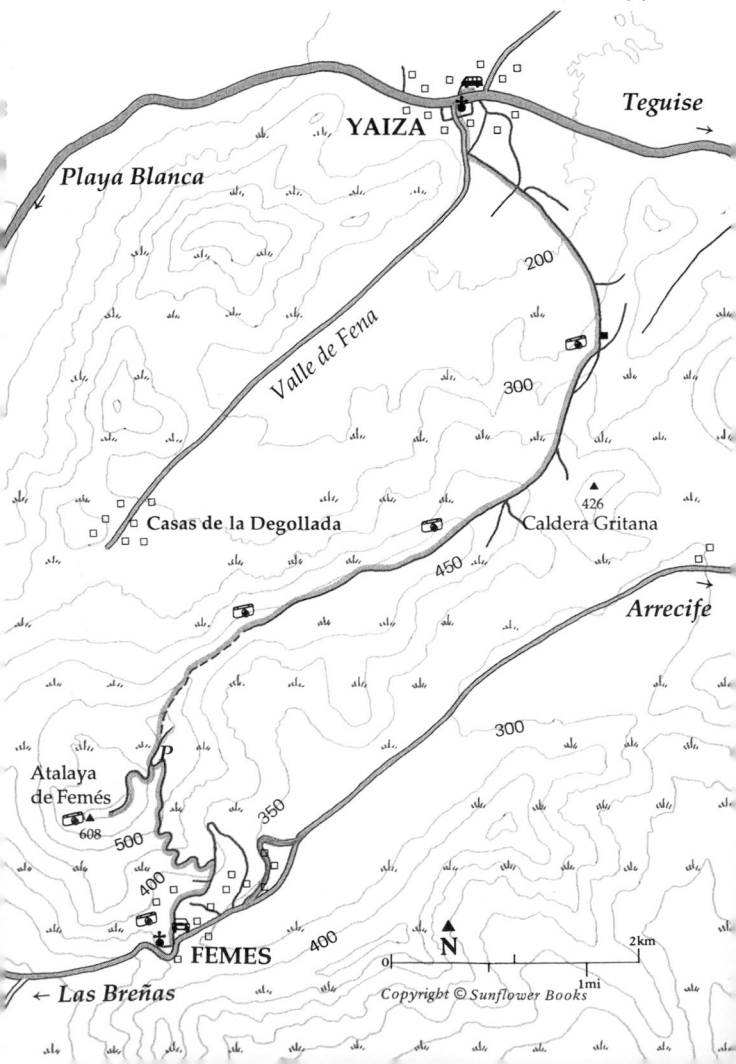

On the climb to the Atalaya de Femés we overlook La Degollada, a small village nestled in a tucked-away valley of the Ajaches hills. The setting for Picnic 7 is nearby.

reappearing again to meet the Atalaya de Femés track, at just under **1h**. Continue up to the right. Seven minutes up, you reach the summit, where a stupendous view awaits you. The remote (for this island!) little village of Femés lies straight below, huddled around the pass that descends to the Rubicón plain. Fuerteventura and Lobos fill in the backdrop. And from up here you can almost count the colourful volcanoes of Timanfaya. On the other side of the transmitter station, you look down onto Las Breñas, stretching along a raised shelf of cultivation that steps off onto the Rubicón.

Descending to Femés is straightforward. Follow the track all the way down to the first fork-off right, and then remain on this track to the village square (25min down). Hopefully you'll be handsomely repaid with a memorable sunset. Allow one hour to return to Yaiza from the summit. In Yaiza, the bus stop is just at the pedestrian crossing north of the plaza.

8 LA HOYA • EL CONVENTO • LA HOYA

Distance: 13km/8mi; 2h30min

Grade: flat and easy, except for the final descent to El Convento, which is vertiginous and dangerous if wet (but this may be omitted)

Equipment: stout shoes with grip (for the descent to El Convento, otherwise comfortable shoes will suffice), sunhat, suncream, cardigan, raingear, picnic, plenty of water, swimwear

How to get there: Playa Blanca- 🚌 to La Hoya (departures from Arrecife and Puerto del Carmen)
To return: 🚌 from La Hoya

If you're tired of picnicking at the beach and eating sandwiches 'à la grit', then this coastal walk, with its superb unvisited rock pools may be just what you're looking for. Beyond Playa de Janubio you follow a jagged, rocky coastline. There are no more beaches (or people), only natural rock pools — pools to suit all the family — hidden on the lava shelves that jut out into the sea. El Convento is the name given to the impressive sea cave at the end of the walk. It's a beautiful stretch of coastline, only frequented by the local fishermen.

Leave the bus at La Hoya (the junction for Las Breñas) and **start the walk:** follow the road south to the Mirador de las Salinas turn-off, less than **10min** along. It's the first track forking off to the right. Head out to the *mirador*— a point that hangs out over the salt pans and lagoon. From here you have a bird's-eye view over the multitude of tiny white squares of salt and the evaporation ponds that divide up the basin floor, leaving it with a sunset-pink glow. The dark green lagoon enhances this fine setting (see photograph page 61). This particular *salina* (salt pan) produces one-third of Lanzarote's salt. Ornithologists will be happy to know that this is a popular destination for migratory birds as well, and you can expect to find: teal, the cattle egret and little egret (on rare occasions); the grey heron and storks (from time to time); plovers, lapwing, and sparrow hawks (more commonly). Notice also the few derelict windmills down in the basin; these were used for pumping the seawater into the ponds.

The top of the plateau is bare and dusty. From above the lagoon we continue on further south, circling the top of the basin. When you come to the edge of a small but deep ravine (a couple of minutes from the *mirador*), clamber down the steep rocky face at the mouth of it. Take care, it's gravelly. A two-minute descent (possibly on all fours) drops you down onto the basin floor, near the lagoon. Follow the track over on your left to leave the basin. You'll pass by a shed and below a house, to exit through a chained barrier. Come onto the beach track at just over **20min**. Playa de Janubio sweeps around the shoreline below you. From here we head south (left) along the edge of the sea plain, following trails the fishermen use.

Our continuation is a very faint track that lies across the beach track. It begins half a minute up to your left. Soon you'll see the remains of the old Playa Blanca route — a raised stone-built piece of road — below you. Keep close to the sea, so that you don't miss any of those alluring *charcos* (pools) and, where possible, scale down over the rock to check them out. You'll soon discover one that will steal an hour or two of your time. Your own private pool, too!

Along modest cliffs, you follow paths or just plough over the loose lava, and now and then you join up with a stretch of track. If you tire of floundering over all this rocky terrain, head inland for a minute or two and follow the main track along, keeping parallel to the coast. Soon you're looking straight across the stone-strewn Rubicón

The jagged coastline south of the saltpans of Janubio. Beryl-green pools lie ensconced in the low shelves that jut out into the sea. (Car tour 2, Picnic 8; see also photograph page 61.)

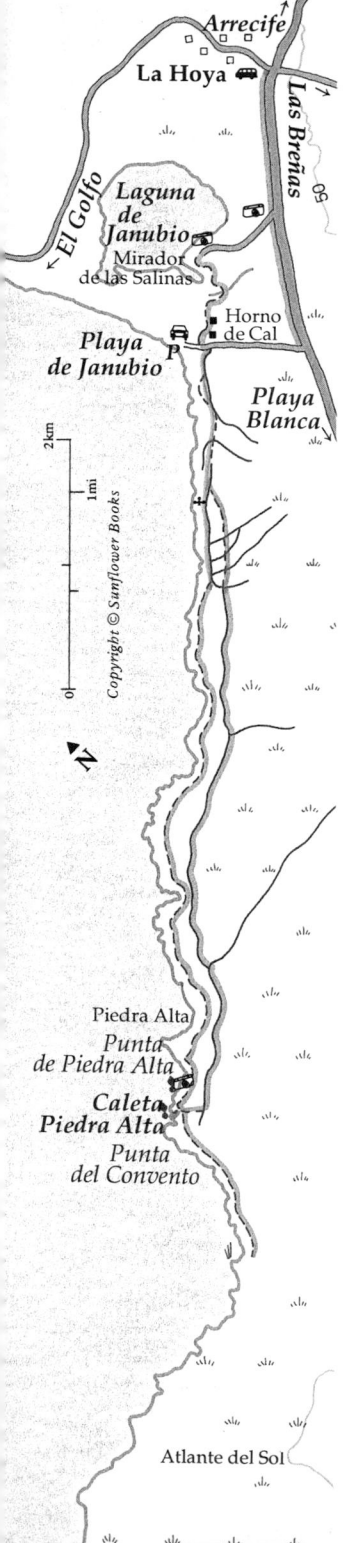

plain to the pointed Ajache hills. In the distance, further along the coast, the abandoned *urbanización* of Atlante del Sol bares itself. Las Breñas is the village you soon see strung out along the edge of an elevated plateau that steps back off this one. The landscape is still and lifeless, and without a drop of colour.

At **35min** into the walk you pass a wooden cross. Stretches of the coastal lava resemble cobblestone paving. About fifteen minutes beyond the cross you begin finding the best pools. So keep an eye out for them. The sea churns up against the shelf, replenishing these pools: obviously, swimming *isn't* recommended in bad weather or when the sea is rough.

At **45min** spot a sea-shelf (from the *edge* of the plain) with a number of pools embedded in it. Two minutes of scrambling over rocks and boulders brings you down to them. This is an excellent spot for children, and the pools are also deep enough for adults. A little over five minutes later, there is another vast shelf with more inviting pools. Finally, a few minutes past this spot, you will find a magnificent solitary pool. All of these emerald-green waterholes are simply irresistible....

Attention is needed at about **1h10min**: Shortly after turning inland (behind a small 'dip') to avoid a mass of lava rock, we pass a cement geographical peg that stands on a point to our right. Here we scramble over all the rock, to the top of the cliffs, for a dramatic coastal overlook. Two inviting green pools lie in what appears to be an inaccessible shelf, immediately below. Behind the pools stands an enormous cave — El Convento — with a

The salt pans of Janubio

'cloistered' entrance opening back into the face of the cliff. A smaller cave sits to its right. Now the problem is: how do we get there?

The safest way down is just beyond the second cave, some three to four minutes round the top of the cliff. You pass over some interesting rock formations, resembling large fragments of broken crockery. Straight off this area of rock, you drop down onto 'lumps' of lava. Meters to the right (and close to the edge of the cliff!), a nose of rock reveals itself. Locating it requires a bit of scouting about. Descend here *with care!* All fours are needed, and this descent is only recommended for *very* surefooted walkers! *Also note: before venturing down, make sure the breakers aren't crashing over the shelf!* When the sea is calm, there is no danger.

This is a superb and sheltered spot to spend the rest of the day. A blow hole lies a further fifteen minutes along the coast, if you can summon up the energy. It's more noticeable for its noise than the spray of water. Find it on a sea shelf set in the 'U' of the next bay along. The noise gives it away.

The return section of the walk is much easier on the feet: we follow a track that lies just a couple of minutes back off the top of the cliff — slightly inland from the path. Heading back, you get a good view of the Golfo crater — a prominant orange-coloured cone that rises up off the seashore. Remain on the track for the next forty minutes or so, keeping along the coast. Ignore all turn-offs inland. You'll cross several other tracks. Just before reaching the beach track you'll be traipsing across a rocky hillside.

Above the beach, continue up the track to the right and, on the main road, turn left to the junction for La Hoya and your bus stop (1h05min back from El Convento).

9 PLAYA BLANCA • PLAYA DE PAPAGAYO • BARRANCO PARRADO • MACIOT • PLAYA BLANCA

Distance: 28km/17.5mi; 5h

Grade: fairly strenuous because of its length. Total ascent is some 300m/1015ft. There is no shade en route, and it can be *very* hot — so keep this walk for cool overcast days.

Equipment: comfortable shoes or walking boots, cardigan, sunhat, suncream, raingear, picnic, plenty of water, swimwear

How to get there: 🚌 to Playa Blanca (departures from Arrecife and Puerto del Carmen)
To return: 🚌 from Playa Blanca

Short walk: Playa Blanca—Playa de Papagayo—Playa Blanca (2h20min; easy)

Sooner or later you'll discover the island's most beautiful beaches — those east of Playa Blanca, of which Playa de Papagayo is the best known. All are accessible by track, but we meander along the jutting coastline, dipping down into each of these delightful beaches, sampling them as we go. You can bet your boots they'll lure you back another day. With the last of the beaches behind you, you won't see another soul. The landscape is sliced up by ravines and hidden valleys, shut off from the rest of the island by a wall of high hills.

Arrecife

Playa Blanca

urbanización

Playa Blanca

Salinas del Berrugo

Punta del Aguila

Castillo de las Coloradas

Playa de Afe

Playa Mujeres

Playa de los Pozos

Playa de Papagayo

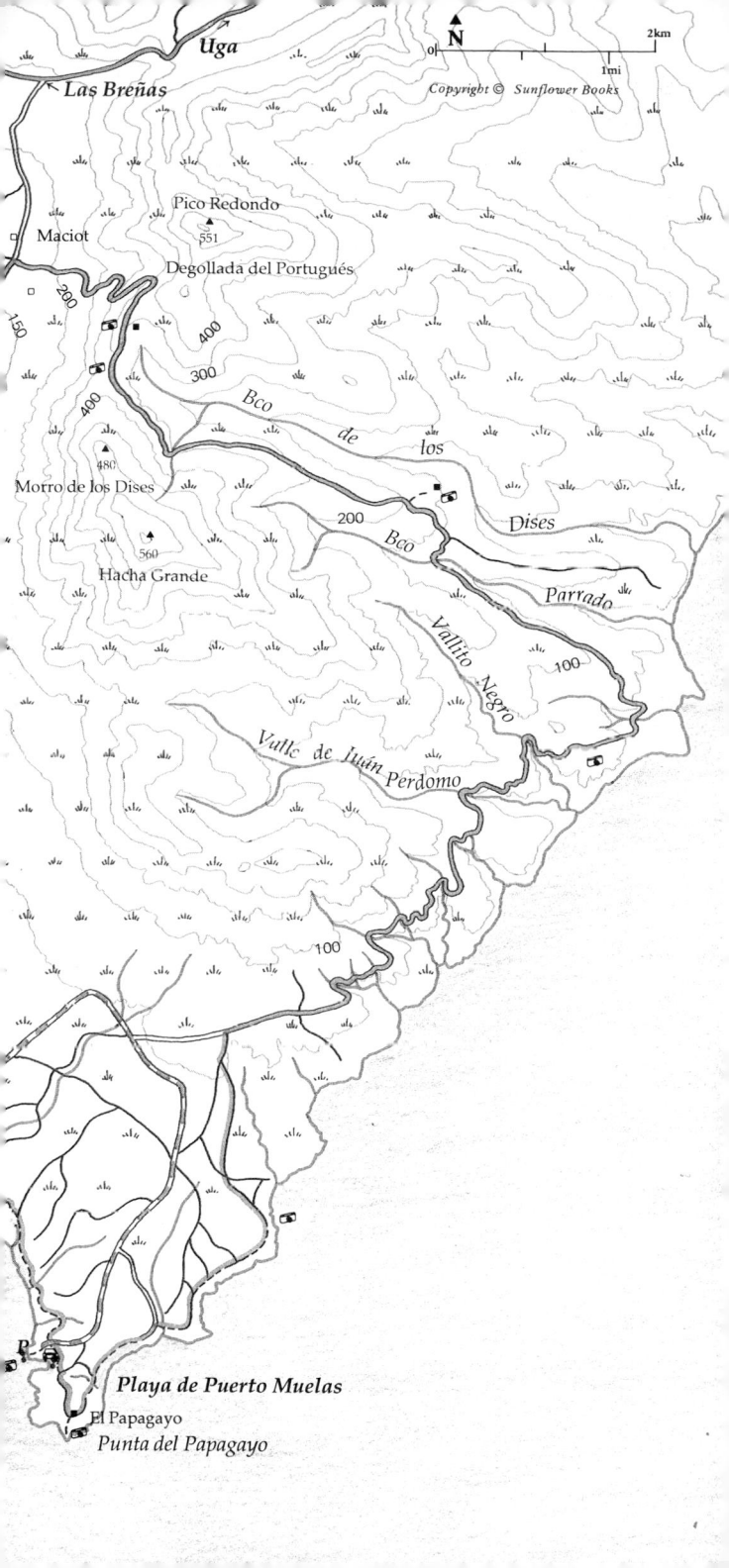

Uga

Las Breñas

N
0 ___ 2km
1mi

Copyright © Sunflower Books

Pico Redondo
▲ 551

Maciot

Degollada del Portugués

200

150

400

300

Bco

de

los

400

Morro de los Dises
▲480

200

Bco

Dises

▲560

Parrado

Hacha Grande

Vallito Negro

100

Valle de Juan Perdomo

100

Playa de Puerto Muelas

P

El Papagayo
Punta del Papagayo

Lanzarote's loveliest beaches, east of Playa Blanca (Picnic 9)

An eyesore of development chewing up the coastline takes up the first half hour of our walk, and there are more such developments on the drawing board. Let's hope that the César Manriques of the island save this unique stretch of coastline. A new road is in the pipeline for Playa de Papagayo, so the map may not be 100% accurate — however, the route is very straightforward. **Start off** by

Camels, once beasts of burden and an important part of the rural scene, lead a much more leisurely life these days ... carrying tourists to the famous Montaña del Fuego. This camel train is homeward-bound.

following the road heading east through the resort.When the asphalt road ends at a T-junction, bear right to follow a gravel road along the coast. Some **20min** en route a detour takes us up to a well-restored circular castle tower (Castillo de las Coloradas), bearing the date 1769. To reach it, leave the track/road just after passing a little house near the sea; follow a faint track up to the tower. Off this headland you have a good view back to Playa Blanca and towards the superb beaches scooped out of the open bay on your left which culminates in Punta de Papagayo. Then a tarred road returns us to the track.

Turn right along it and head up through a large *urbanización* (under construction). Then head down to the beach, the Playa de Afe, just over the hill. Walk along the beach to your left. This stony beach is the ugly duckling of the *playas*. At the end of it a path takes you up (with a slight scramble) to the sea-plain above, where you find a clear path over to Playa Mujeres. Low spiny *Launaea* lies scattered across the plain. Wherever you find *Launaea* there's usually *cosco* nearby. *Cosco* turns a vivid wine colour under drought conditions (see *Landscapes of Fuerteventura*, page 40), and great colonies of it stain the inclines. The fruit of this plant was used to make a substitute *gofio* (normally a roasted corn flour), and was used as a thickening agent in soups, etc.

Some **45min** into the walk the unspoilt Playa Mujeres is in sight. This lovely open beach stretches across the mouth of a shallow *barranco*.El Papagayo, the only sign of civilisation out here, is the handful of derelict buildings near the point. Your path drops down into a small gravelly *barranco* and mounts a faint track which leads you down onto the golden sandy beach. You look back into the windswept hills of Los Ajaches. Near the end of the beach scale the sandy bank to remount the crest — a steep, slippery two-minute climb on sand, followed by loose gravel. Continuing along the top of the crest, you dip in and out of small *barrancos* which empty out into concealed coves below.

Playa de los Pozos is the next of the larger beaches. Straight after crossing a track, you clamber down a narrow streambed to reach it. Ascend the goats' path that edges around the hillside at the end of the beach, and once again you're above the sea. If the way appears vertiginous, scramble up onto the plain straight up from the beach. More enticing coves reveal themselves. Most days you'll find they're occupied; this coastline is well and truly 'discovered' — but, fortunately, far from crowded. Soon the old settlement of Papagayo reappears on the crest of the ridge ahead; its crumbled stone buildings leave one assuming that it's uninhabited. Circling behind a couple of coves you reach the top of the crest (**1h10min**) — and find that, to the contrary, El Papagayo *is* inhabited ... by hippies. A rust-brown and deep mauve-coloured rocky promontory separates the two dazzling coves on either side of you. From here you have a striking view of the smooth-faced inland hills, as well as along the string of beaches you've just visited (see photograph page 64). If you're only doing the Short walk, you'll have plenty of time to sample these paradisial beaches and coves; otherwise, you'll only have time for a couple of them.

Continuing on, follow the path curving around the walls of Playa de Papagayo. You look down onto the beach and a number of tents fastened to the face of the hill. Ice-plants and *cosco* patch the slope. (If this path looks unnerving, make your way around via the top of the crest.) Shortly meet a track from your left and follow it out to Punta del Papagayo. It passes a pillbox a couple of minutes along and then swings sharply back left. The point is just beyond the shelter. *Don't* go too near to the edge of the cliffs on windy days! Fuerteventura is now closer than ever, and the dark 'pimply' island of Lobos is made more prominent by the sand dunes of Corralejo in the background. Back to your left you can see Puerto del Carmen and Arrecife — a vast expanse of white trimming the sloping sea-plain. A staggered chain of cone-shaped hills runs down the centre of the island.

A few minutes below the pillbox (at about **1h20min**) the track fizzles out onto yet another beach — Playa de Puerto Muelas. This secluded beach is the most popular out here. Could the fact that it's the (unofficial) nudist beach have something to do with it? Five minutes along the beach (trying not to look left or right), reach the carpark. Follow the track north to the next cove, a minute over, and then ascend to the top of the cliffs beyond it. Pieces of track lead you along these cliffs. Ten minutes from the last beach you come onto a clearer track and overlook a rocky cove set at the mouth of a deep ravine. Here we turn up left, keeping straight up (bear left at the fork you encounter and pass through an intersection), until we meet a T-junction (at about **1h50min**).

Bearing right at the junction we now sidle along the hills, disappearing further out 'into the sticks'. No more beaches, no more people ... but perhaps a goatherd and a handful of goats. Ignoring all tracks that fork off left and right, we remain on a generally even contour. Gradually ascending, we look straight off the sloping shelf onto the sea. The way curves back into a number of *barrancos* that slice inland, and soon it's no longer passable by vehicles (from this side). Some **2h20min** en route, drop down into a good-sized gulley and cross a wide gravelly streambed. The countryside can be surprisingly green out here in winter and spring. Still no sign of life, nor any trees ... a desolate spot indeed.

Tías comes into full view, its elevated slopes speckled with white buildings. The surrounding hills have subsided into a gentle rolling landscape. A brief descent takes you down to another *barranco* crossing. Now the hard work begins — a 60-minute uphill slog follows. We wind our way up into the largest of the valleys so far encountered. Dandelions and *Echium* add their golds and purples to the spring greenery. Some five minutes uphill from the streambed crossing, come to an intersection and bear left. A few minutes later, you'll see a shepherds' crumbled outpost on a rocky outcrop above the track. On a windy day it serves as a good picnic shelter. There's also a large colony of ice plants here. This plant was once traded for its soda content. Pico Redondo (551m/1800ft) is the peak rising up out of the next valley over on your right. Nearer the pass, you encounter the first trees — some rather scrawny examples of *Solanaceae* (the tobacco family) — scattered along the side of the road.

A fantastic viewpoint (where you're often hit by a gale-force wind), awaits you when you cross the pass ... or are blown over it ... and descend to the Playa Blanca wasteland. You look back down the valley and over the stone-covered Rubicón plain that fans out across the southwestern corner of the island. Below sits the tiny hamlet of Maciot — a manicured patch of gardens completely lost in this dark, dismal corner. Playa Blanca is to your left and El Faro (the lighthouse) de la Punta Pechiguera to the right of it. A goats' pen made of 44 gallon drums sits at the top of the pass (**3h35min** en route). Dropping quickly now, you twist down the sheer escarpment. Twenty minutes down, exit onto the gravel Las Breñas/Femés—Playa Blanca road and turn left along it. Keep straight on after the cement works and join the main road just above Playa Blanca. Two minutes down to the left, reach a roundabout and the bus stop.

 Index

Geographical names comprise the only entries in this index; for other entries, see Contents on page 3. **Bold-face** type indicates a photograph; *italic* type indicates a map reference.

 # Stop Press

IMPORTANT
We frequently receive letters from people who say that Noel Rochford's walking times are misleading. In his Walking Introduction, Noel always warns readers that he is a 'very fit, very fast walker'. Unfortunately many people don't read the introduction. Probably one of the reasons for the fast timings is that Noel always walks alone … just what we ask you not to do!

We urge all readers to compare their pace to Noel's on one or two short walks before setting out on longer hikes.

WALKING MAPS
Scales: Sorry! The scales are incorrect on the walking maps: for '1mi' read '1km' and for '2km' read '1mi'.

FERRIES
The ferry service between Lanzarote and Fuerteventura is much improved. Ferry Betancuria supplied the following timetable in 1993:
depart Playa Blanca (Lanzarote) for Fuerteventura 09.00, 11.00, 15.30, 18.00*
*19.00 from April to October
depart Corralejo (Fuerteventura) for Lanzarote 08.00, 10.00 14.30, 17.00*
*18.00 from April to October

BUSES
The bus station in Arrecife has been moved to the Valterra area. It is on Calle Velacho (not shown on our plan). From the 'D' exit symbol on our plan, walk 300m/yds northeast along Calle Galdós (shown in grey): Calle Velacho will then be on your right. Turn right, to find the new station 150m/yds along on your right, opposite Calle Botavera.

All buses still stop at the old station, as well as on Playa, next to the Gran Hotel.

Many bus times have changed; be sure to pick up a new timetable from the new bus station in Arrecife!

CAR TOURS
Tour 1: The cactus garden is now open.

WALKS

Although Noel is a very fast walker, his books are often used by elderly people: 'We hire a car and do parts of walks. My comments are aimed at the fairly elderly, and would make good picnic suggestions, too. Walk 4: Parked just below wireless (?) station on Peñas del Chache and walked to the Ermita de las Nieves and beyond. (We could also have walked in the other direction without losing much height.) Walk 5: We drove to Playa de la Madera (no difficulty driving slowly along this track) and walked along a clearly-marked cliff path southwards for a couple of miles. Very spectacular, especially the narrow clefts in the lava cliffs. Walk 6: Our favourite, from Uga to the turn-off to Montana Guardilama, with the people working the vines and magnificent views.' (User, 1991)

Walk 3 (alternative): The narrow lane that forks off left 5min beyond the second junction has been asphalted all the way up to a race track near the cliff-tops. The remainder of the walk is along a track, which continues past the race track turn-off. (User, 1993)

Walk 6: The farm track at the start of the walk is now metalled... The 'faint' track to Guardilama (at 40min) is now very clear. At the summit of Guardilama there is a trig point...After 1h25min, you may have difficulty following the route to the G720 because of building works. (User, 1992)

Walk 7: The track off to the left, cutting across the valley (page 55) is now tarred.

A user recommends doing the walk in reverse, which would mean taking a taxi to Femés to begin. After the initial steep ascent to the *atalaya*, the rest is all downhill. Also check in advance that the buses returning to Arrecife pass through the village of Uga.